OUR SPEAKER TODAY:
A GUIDE TO EFFECTIVE LECTURING

Dr Allan Gaw has been lecturing and giving presentations for over 25 years and thinks that by now he might have learned a few secrets about how it should be done. Having been to Medical School in the early 1980s he certainly gained a very good grounding on how it should *not* be done. In the last two and half decades he has, through observing the best and by sometimes painful trial and error, developed a simple and foolproof system for the preparation and delivery of a good lecture. This book presents a distillation of that experience and will be invaluable to anyone having to prepare their first 'talks' as well as those who may have been lecturing for years but are still struggling to find it an enjoyable experience. This is a book packed with practical advice and as the, often simple, secrets are revealed the reader will become convinced that it will never be so daunting again.

Allan Gaw, MD, PhD, FRCPath, FFPM, PGCert Med Ed is Director of Operations at the Glasgow Clinical Research Facility. He is the author or editor of 15 books mostly on the subjects of Clinical Biochemistry, Cardiovascular Research, Lipid Metabolism and Clinical Trials. You can learn more about him and his work at **www.allangaw.com**

Further resources related to this book can be found on its linked website **www.academic-skills.com**

D1439965

OTHER WORKS BY THE AUTHOR

Gaw, A and Shepherd, J. *Coronary Risk Factors Measurement and Management* Martin Dunitz, London, 1999.

Gaw, A and Shepherd, J. (eds). *Atherosclerosis and Lipid Annual 2001* Martin Dunitz, London, 2001.

Gaw, A. *Statins in General Practice* 2nd edition Martin Dunitz, London, 2003.

Gaw, A and Shepherd J. *Statins and Stroke Prevention* Science Press, Tokyo, 2003.

Gaw, A and Shepherd, J. (eds). *Atherosclerosis and Lipid Annual 2003* Martin Dunitz Taylor Francis Group, London, 2003.

Gaw, A, Packard, CJ and Shepherd, J. (eds). *Statins: the HMG CoA reductase inhibitors in perspective* 2nd edition Martin Dunitz, London, 2004.

Lindsay, GM and Gaw, A. (eds). *Coronary Heart Disease Prevention: A Handbook for the Health-care Team* 2nd edition Harcourt Brace, Edinburgh, 2004.

Gaw, A, Murphy, MA, Cowan, RA, O'Reilly, D St J, Stewart, MJ, and Shepherd J. *Clinical Biochemistry An Illustrated Colour Text* 4th edition Elsevier, Edinburgh, 2008.

Gaw, A. *Trial by Fire: Lessons from the History of Clinical Trials.* SA Press, Glasgow, 2009.

OUR SPEAKER TODAY:
A GUIDE TO EFFECTIVE LECTURING

Allan Gaw

For Michelle –

With best wishes

Allan Gaw

2016

First published 2010
By SA Press
4 Birkdale Wood, Westerwood, G68 0GY, UK

Printed and bound in the United Kingdom by Clydeside Press

British Library Cataloguing in Publication Data
A catalogue record for this book is available from the British Library

ISBN 978-0-9563242-1-4

For Moira

CONTENTS

FOREWORD

The two best lectures I ever attended were very different. One was given in Glasgow by a visiting academic from Toronto who told the story of the Discovery of Insulin. The other was given in Dallas by an American entomologist who described his work on how ants found their way back to their anthills after being out foraging. One was an historical review and analysis, and one was a detailed exposition of laboratory science. My selection of these two examples for special mention raises an important question: what was it about these lectures that made them so memorable? In terms of content they certainly had almost nothing in common, but where they did overlap was in the overwhelming enthusiasm of the presenters for their subjects, the obvious meticulous preparation that had gone into them and the sheer style of their delivery. Great lectures are relatively few and far between in my experience – that's two in 30 years – but regrettably bad lectures abound. Unfortunately, many lecturers, even if they have been working in their field for years, struggle to get beyond the barely mediocre.

The good lecture is more common, but not as common as it should be. This simple fact was the prompt for the writing of this book, because I firmly believe that any lecturer can deliver a good talk if they try. I wrote this book in order to help those completely new to lecturing and presenting, as well as those who have been doing it for years. For both groups lecturing should be simple, straightforward and enjoyable both for them and their audience. The rules are simple and easy to follow and this book is written on the premise that it really isn't rocket science. (Even if, by chance, you happen to be a solid fuel booster specialist it isn't, or at least lecturing about it shouldn't be.)

But let's not just settle for good - some will go even further and, who knows, perhaps end up being mentioned in the foreword of some future book on presentation skills as a paradigm of excellence.

Lectures should not be boring, perfunctory, and ill-prepared or delivered as an afterthought. We should not be made to feel grateful that a 'great speaker' has deigned to grace us with his or her presence. Nor should we have to struggle to understand what is being said or strain to see what is being shown. Lecturers, if they wish to call themselves that, should do the necessary work before, during and after a lecture to ensure its quality. This book is not about how to give a mediocre lecture – it's about how to give a good, maybe even a great, lecture, and one that is certainly useful and memorable for the audience. This book is about being an engaged professional not a distant expert; about being a teacher, not simply a performer.

Please don't read this book if you already think you are good enough. You probably aren't, but with that attitude I am not sure I can teach you anything. Do read this book if, no matter how long you have been giving talks, you think you may have something to learn. That openness to new possibilities means we can work together and all the mistakes I've made don't have to be repeated by someone else. You will, I hope, enjoy the book – it's meant to be entertaining - and you may end up a better teacher. At least you will have had a chance to think about how you lecture and what you might do differently next time you are asked to give a talk.

ACKNOWLEDGEMENTS

The contents of this book are based on 30 years of listening to lectures and 25 years of giving them. Without free and unfettered access to a long list of truly terrible lecturers I would not have thought this book necessary, and nor would I have had the determination to do better in my own talks. But, as well as learning from the worst I have also been blessed with the best and it is those teachers that I wish to acknowledge - in particular, Jim Shepherd, Chris Packard and most of all Bob Cowan, one of my first lecturers at University, always the best and, I am proud to say, also a good friend and co-author.

The editorial team at SA Press deserves special mention for without their drive and attention to detail this book would surely never have been finished. In particular, I must thank my editor, Moira Mungall, who says the harshest of things in the softest of voices and always makes small suggestions that result in big improvements. Drafts of the text were read and corrected by Eleanor Dinnett, Liz Ronald and Liz Tolmie. I thank them for all the time they spent, but emphasise that any mistakes or pieces of clumsy writing that remain are entirely my own. The designer David Tolmie was responsible for the cover and for polishing my cartoons throughout the book. Liz Ronald was also responsible for helping take the manuscript from its first drafts to the finished book you are reading now.

Ladies and gentlemen, thank you.

INTRODUCTION:

SEAGULLS, TARTS AND SPENCER TRACY

Giving a 'talk' is a key skill for most professionals. For some, such as college lecturers, it will be a daily task; for others it will only be an occasional duty. For some it will be easy; for others it will be their worst nightmare. Whatever your professional role and whatever stage you are at, being able to give a clear, effective and informative presentation is something that needs to be worked at. Few of us are naturals – even those we think of as born speakers have had to hone and develop their skills through a lot of practice.

So we have established that it's important and that it's worth spending a little time on. Are there rules? Can one be taught to lecture? Is there a recipe for success? Of course there is and in this book I will take you through the list of ingredients and along the way I will share with you many tricks of the trade.

First of all, you have to ask yourself a question: what kind of lecturer do you want to be? Believe it or not you do have a choice and there is a range to choose from. It comes down to style. It was Oscar Wilde who said that in matters of grave importance, style, rather than sincerity, is the vital thing. Now Oscar is renowned to have been rather a good lecturer and he probably followed his own advice and maximized on style. But, what we are talking about here is not necessarily whether you choose a flamboyant cape, a feathered fedora or even a green carnation. Rather, what we are concerned with is your whole approach to the business of giving a lecture.

Whether you are new to presenting or are an old hand, but have always found it a challenge, I suggest beginning with simplicity. Some think simplicity will betray them, leading the chairman, the other speakers and the audience to conclude that their work itself is simple, and therefore lightweight, just because they are explaining it in a simple fashion. In fact, simplicity is appreciated by audiences the world over. Indeed it was Leonardo Da Vinci who said: "Simplicity is the ultimate sophistication" although admittedly he did say it backwards and written in code. Clear, concise messages unadorned by the complexity that is possible through modern technologies, delivered in a simple unassuming style will win the day. As you gain experience and confidence you will develop your own style, but this should never be at the expense of the simplicity with which you began. Great lecturers have style, but they also have clarity and above all, simplicity. Never mistake simplicity for lack of content.

DIFFERENT KINDS OF LECTURER

So, what kind of lecturer might you be? Over the years I, like most of you, have seen them all, and I have six categories as follows:

POWERPOINT VICTIMS

These are members of the 'more-is-more' school of lecturing. Remember, just because you can do it does not mean you should. This goes for many aspects of life, but is especially true of Microsoft PowerPoint. This software package and others like it, such as Macintosh Keynotes, are remarkable tools that have transformed the way we construct lectures and create the visuals we use to support them. But, they offer an almost bewildering array of fonts, colours, entrance effects and quite literally bells and whistles should you want them.

It is tempting to introduce interesting effects and perhaps a different background in every slide just for variety's sake, and perhaps having each word spin in from the top left hand corner of the slide, and have each letter of your title in a different colour or even a different font – to make it all more eye-catching. Trust me – it does not. Instead, it is irritating, distracting and does exactly the opposite to your intention of engaging your audience – they will be turned off. Don't spoil a clear presentation on your important work by clothing it in an amazing Technicolor Dream Coat of a slide set.

PHONERS

"Phoning-it-in" is an expression from the acting profession which denotes those who put minimal effort into a performance and might as well have 'phoned it in'. In lecturing, the same happens – minimal effort from the busy professional or disinterest from a so-called expert.

I was once given an effusive introduction from a chairman who concluded by saying after he listed my publications almost one by one, my honours and awards – even, it seemed at the time, my inside leg measurements – that the greatest honour of all and the pinnacle of my career was to be invited to speak at their lunchtime meeting in Stoke-on-Trent. Now, he was being funny and indeed got the laugh. But, there was a serious point. Sometimes, if you are used to travelling on an international circuit speaking to large sophisticated audiences, the prospect of speaking to a small local group might lull you into thinking that less effort is needed. Notions of pearls before swine might enter your head; you might think I'll just phone this one in. Don't. First because you are a professional and if you have been asked to speak - even to five sales reps on a wet Wednesday in the middle of nowhere - and you have accepted, they deserve your best. Also, and equally importantly, just because it's not the Oxford Union or the keynote address of the International Society of Cardiology, does not mean their expectations will not be high and their questions searching. I have never yet been asked a question at a big meeting that I couldn't at least attempt to answer, but I have been asked by nurses, medical students and even, on one memorable occasion, by the lady who washed the glassware in the lab, questions that have floored me.

SEAGULLS

As birds, seagulls are renowned for flying in, dropping what they drop and flying out again. Can you see the comparison with some lecturers? They usually arrive at the last minute, of course have not had the time to have their slides loaded properly by the AV technician and routinely have to leave before the panel discussion so they can catch the earliest possible plane to their next destination – not usually home, but the next symposium where they will repeat their seagull impression. Now, there is nothing wrong with being busy and in demand, but you need at least to give the impression that you are glad to be here and that the time you are spending belongs to the audience – after all they are busy too and they have shown up. This approach stems from arrogance and the resulting lectures, which are often of mediocre quality, stem from lack of thought and preparation.

TARTS

Yes, you have met them for they abound in different professional groupings and they are everywhere. You will meet them again and again in your particular field for that's what they do. They have turned lecturing into a cash-cow and encouraged by industry or public bodies they are travellers on "the circuit". Now there are many speakers who are popular lecturers and who travel widely, but who could never be described as tarts. The particular brand of speaker I am thinking of here would turn up for the opening of an envelope and would be happy to take a fee for doing so. An interesting subset of Tarts is that of the Pinocchios. "I've got no strings" sang Pinocchio. Some lecturers are keen to let everyone know that they are the same, i.e. no controlling influences or conflicts of interest. The problem is, no one should have, but those who feel the need to say it – repeatedly – are usually the ones who do. Routinely you will find such speakers at industry sponsored symposia where they are being paid to take part and as such they feel the need to emphasise their impartiality. Such speakers often give their audiences little credit. Most audiences can detect inappropriate partiality in a presentation from the back stalls. Although fond of stating how unbiased their lectures are you will often see them at the next meeting you attend speaking on behalf of another industry sponsor and happily espousing the merits of a new product. Tarts do it for money and money alone – they can be bought, often rather cheaply in my experience – and their reputations become as flimsy as their lectures.

CELEBRITIES

The popularity of some lecturers hinges not on their ability to lecture, but on their fame or celebrity. Public lectures are a good source of such speakers. The poster will announce the visit of a noteworthy to your institution and you will be tempted to attend to see and hear the great one. Unfortunately, when you turn up the speaker turns out to be reading from a sheaf of poorly prepared notes or using slides that the local kindergarten class could have prepared better. You are disappointed, but you are still in the same room as someone whom you otherwise respect, perhaps even revere, and you may forgive them and even report that it was worth attending, thus perpetuating the myth.

Some academics also fall into this category. Perhaps they have written a highly respected book or conducted a major study. To have them in the flesh is enough to attract a large audience. Whether they can actually speak fluently and deliver a coherent lecture is almost beside the point.

Unfortunately, unless you are famous and can dazzle your audience with your celebrity you will need to try a little harder. That same audience will be less forgiving of the failings of an unknown.

SPENCER TRACY'S

Spencer Tracy was an American actor; some would say a great actor. He starred in classic films such as *Adam's Rib*, *Inherit the Wind* and *Guess Who's Coming to Dinner?* He was not a lecturer, but his approach to his craft was one that we would do well to emulate. He said, "Know your lines, show up on time, and don't bump into the furniture." I rather suspect Mr. Tracy knew what he was talking about and this is the kind of lecturer I think we should aspire to be – at least it is my aspiration. I want to be seen as the consummate professional, who knows what I am there to do, has prepared well, and delivers a good lecture without redress to gimmickry. I want to attend to the needs of my audience and at all times keep it simple. No prima donna, no condescending expert, no fumbling amateur – just quality and professionalism. Spencer Tracy was never short of work – nor will you be if you acquire a reputation as this kind of lecturer.

Clearly I have had fun here in describing the kinds of lecturers I don't like, but I must reiterate my main point: there are different approaches to lecturing and you do have the power to choose which kind you become. Much of this approach is to do with attitude rather than technical ability. Most of this book will be about the technical side of giving a talk and in many ways that is the easy part. What will set you apart from others as a good, maybe even a great, lecturer will be your attitude to your audience and to the task in hand. If you think lecturing is something to be endured it will look like that. If you think your audience does not deserve your time they will realise that. If, however, you are enthusiastic about lecturing and are willing to work at it as a mark of respect for your audience, your efforts will be acknowledged and, what is more, you will begin to enjoy lecturing and your audiences will be eager to hear more.

The very fact that you are reading this book bodes well. For if you were uninterested and felt it was all rather beneath you I suspect you would not have come this far. So, from this point onwards I will assume that you want to be a better lecturer and that you would prefer to be a "Spencer Tracy" rather than a Tart or a Seagull. That decision, now made, is the most important step towards being a more effective lecturer. Now, we have to deal with the rest.

THE FORMAT OF THIS BOOK

I have divided the process of devising and delivering a lecture into a series of steps roughly corresponding with the chronological order in which you deal with them. Each of these steps is dealt with in the following chapters. Many of you will want to look at each step in turn and read the book in the order that it is presented. Others may wish to go to an area where they have particular difficulties. As each chapter is written in a largely standalone way this approach does not present a problem. Feel free to dip in and out of the chapters as you wish.

Chapter 1 deals with Preparation. With lecturing, like painting and decorating, the quality of the final product is as much, if not more, to do with preparation as with the actual process of delivery. This chapter is therefore probably the most important in the book and is full of useful tips on how to be a good lecturer before you have even opened your mouth.

Chapters 2, 3 and 4 are about the lecture itself: the Beginning, the Middle and the End. Each of these chapters detail tried and tested strategies for designing and delivering each component of your lecture.

When you thank your audience for their attention your job as a lecturer is not over. In many cases you will then have to answer questions. In Chapter 5 we look at the best approaches to this part of the lecture – a prospect that many new speakers find the most daunting of all.

Most lecturers will employ visual aids, usually in the form of slides to illustrate and signpost their lectures. In Chapter 6 we look in detail at the best way to prepare slides and I present a simple five step approach to ensure they enhance your lecture rather than detract from it.

It would be foolish to think that things always go as planned. Obviously, they do not, but the trick is to have ways at your disposal of coping with disaster or what sometimes seems like disaster. Chapter 7 is my opportunity to highlight the most common banana skins that will be thrown your way and to let you into a few secrets on how to avoid them.

In Chapter 8 we deal with the specific challenges of lecturing in other countries. Many speakers will get the opportunity to speak at international conferences or be fortunate enough to be invited to share their insights and wisdom with people who do not speak English. This is an exciting opportunity both professionally and personally and this chapter ensures you are appropriately prepared.

Lecturing can be a money-making exercise for some and if you are on "the circuit" Chapter 9 will give you useful pointers to ensure you maximize your earnings, and at the same time build your reputation as a professional.

Finally, we bring it all together in Chapter 10, where I present my top tips for a great talk.

I firmly believe the skills associated with lecturing and giving a good talk are transferable. The practical approaches presented in this book apply equally to university lectures, departmental presentations, company reports, and even after-dinner speeches. All will be slightly different with subtly different challenges, but there is more that unites these forms of public speaking than divides them. In the following chapters you will find a range of useful advice born of experience that you can put into practice right away whatever kind of presentation you need to give.

What you will not find in this book is a serious review of the educational literature. This is quite deliberate, as I do not believe that most people approaching lecturing or other forms of public speaking for the first time need, or want, such a background. They do want to know what they can do in practical terms to make it better, easier and more effective. The theoretical basis of education whether viewed from a philosophical or psychological perspective is very important, but I do not think it is what this book should be about. If you do want to read further on those topics there are a number of excellent resources listed in the further reading section at the end of this book, as well as a range of other books and publications I have found useful.

I

PREPARATION:

AVOIDING DISTANT ELEPHANTS

ailing to prepare is preparing to fail – so they, rather irritatingly, say. Irritatingly, because of course they are right and never more so than when it comes to lecturing. Occasionally you will be asked to lecture at alarmingly short notice. The intended speaker has failed to arrive and you happen to be in the wrong place at the wrong time – i.e. in the line of vision of the stressed-out chairman. Those occurrences aside, most of the time you will have time to prepare. You will have been invited weeks, sometimes months in advance and can hardly claim on the day that there was not enough time to prepare. The concept of *distant elephants* comes in here of course. An elephant in the distance seems small and inconsequential, but as it gets closer and finally when you are eye-to-eye - assuming you are as tall as Oscar Hammerstein's lyrical corn - it's a whole different thing. It looms large and imposing and not a little intimidating. Well, invitations to lecture are like that. 'Can you give a talk at our meeting next April?' the voice on the phone asks in November. 'Sure', after all that's months away - plenty of time; no need to worry about it or even think about it at all. Problem is, it's a distant elephant starting to walk slowly but interminably towards you across the pages of your diary as soon as you have said yes, and before you know it the talk is tomorrow, and suddenly there is a really big elephant in the room.

One way to avoid this stress is very simple – when you note the April date in your diary put in some other dates too – your own deadlines. For example, you may put a note in two weeks before to say 'prepare April lecture' and one four weeks before to say 'collect relevant papers for April talk'. The exact prompts will depend on the kind of lecture you are to deliver, but the principle is the same throughout – you need to set aside some time to prepare a lecture. If you walk in unprepared you will look it and will give a poor account of yourself and your work, even if it's a standard lecture you have given before. The reasons for the latter are because every audience and venue is different and part of your preparation will be to consider these as well as preparing the lecture.

In Chapters 2-4 we shall look at the specific elements of the lecture – its beginning, its middle and its end – and will discuss how to construct them. In the remainder of this chapter we shall look at more general considerations.

THE TOPIC

"And what do you want me to cover?" This has never seemed to me to be an unreasonable question to ask of the organizer after you have agreed to speak at their meeting or on their course. Strangely, however, it does seem to prompt a very mixed response. You have presumably been asked to speak on a topic with which you are familiar, but surprisingly organizers sometimes fail to acknowledge this. Often the topic of the presentation is left at best vague and at worst completely undefined. Sometimes they seem so pleased to have filled a slot in their conference programme or their course timetable that they almost don't care what you talk about as long as you show up and have a pulse. Ideally you want to be briefed on the topic you should cover, the level of coverage and of course how long you have to speak for. If it is being left to you to define the topic that's fine but you need to know this, and even if you have a free hand you are still likely to have a defined timeslot on the programme.

At the other extreme, occasionally you will receive extensive briefing notes on your presentation, sometimes so extensive you might wonder why they are asking you to be involved in the lecture at all – the person who has written the "notes" would be as well to give the talk.

Importantly, you should at least be given a title or be able to offer one for approval. Once this is set and the timings worked out you can go ahead with reasonable confidence to construct your lecture.

Sometimes an organizer will expect to have even more control and you will be sent a set of PowerPoint slides, perhaps with accompanying notes and you will be asked to deliver this lecture and no other. This sometimes happens on college courses when you are being asked to give a colleague's lecture, or with overly sensitive commercial organisations who feel the need to control and contain you. My advice is, if at all possible, to resist this approach. Trying to give a lecture using someone else's slides and therefore someone else's take on the topic is difficult; trying to give a good lecture in these circumstances is almost impossible.

THE AUDIENCE

At Medical School we were often confronted with lecturers who would arrive late and flustered and begin not with any introduction, but with a question: "What year are you?" At this point I, and most of my fellow students, would sit back, put our pens down and prepare for a train wreck and an evening spent with the books trying to catch up with what we were supposed to learn in the lecture. We knew from experience that if the lecturer did not even know the academic level of the audience the lecture was unlikely to be of any quality.

As a lecturer you have no excuse for not being prepared in this way. All you have to do is ask a simple question of the organizers. Ideally you should be aware of not only the background of your audience, but how your lecture or series of lectures fits into their course. If your lecture is a standalone presentation to a professional or postgraduate group you should be equally well briefed. If you are not, and often organizers are not sufficiently forthcoming about this, then it is your fault and no one else's. Clearly, the make-up of the audience is critical to the kind of lecture you are to present. Even if the topic is the same, you will not be giving the same lecture to second year medical students as you would to a group of professors of psychiatry. Similarly an internal presentation to your departmental staff is unlikely to be the same as that used for the shareholder meeting.

SPECIAL AUDIENCE GROUPS

Every audience is different and as pointed out above it is important to do your homework on their composition and background knowledge. In addition, there are some audience groups that need some special attention and preparation. I have selected three such groups for special mention here: the disabled, children and lay groups.

DISABLED

Certain forms of disability have to be taken into account. If possible part of knowing your audience should be finding out beforehand if there will be any blind, partially sighted or deaf people in attendance. Blind or partially sighted members of the audience will be able to make little use of your slides or other visual aids, but they can still hear you. If you are aware that there will be visually impaired audience members make sure that your talk can be understood and appreciated without the standard visual back-ups, and try to be sensitive about referring to images in your slides. "As you can see in this slide…" will not mean much.

Deaf members of the audience may be lip reading and it is important that they can clearly see your mouth throughout. This may mean not dimming lights and of course not turning away unnecessarily. Occasionally your lecture may be simultaneously translated into sign language. If this is the case there are a number of issues very similar to those relating to simultaneous translation into another spoken language. These are dealt with in Chapter 8.

CHILDREN

Assuming you are not a school teacher, a Brownie pack leader or a party clown you are probably not used to speaking to groups of children and this presents a new set of challenges. Children are not a homogeneous group and there is big difference in speaking to five year olds and fifteen year olds. In general, however the attention of children is harder to win and to keep, but worth a great deal more than adult audiences when you do. You will have to be even more stimulating, colourful and entertaining than usual and you will also have to be more honest. You will see magic in the eyes of children if you tell them something new and exciting, but you will also see scorn if they think you are being disingenuous. As you may be much more used to speaking to adult audiences, when the invitation comes to speak to children you may be tempted to say no. Don't, say yes instead – for if you can make your subject as exciting to them as it is to you, you may have sown the seed of succession, thus helping ensure that your subject will be in safe hands in the future. The stakes are therefore high and you will have to put in the appropriate effort to ensure the odds are on your side. And, once you have finished your talk you will never again criticise a primary or secondary school teacher who does it all day, everyday.

LAY GROUPS

You may be invited to speak as a specialist to lay groups, i.e. non-specialists. This might come as an invitation from the local Rotary Club, a Board of Trustees of a group that has given you funding, a Parent-Teacher Association, or even the local Cricket Club dinner. Almost everything that has already been set out in this book, as well as what is to follow, applies just as much to these speaking engagements as to student lectures and peer to peer presentations.

The only thing I would add, in case it is necessary to emphasise it, is that lay people are not stupid people. While they will not be familiar with your particular brand of professional jargon, or with the ins and outs of your subject they will often be highly literate professionals in their own right. Never make the mistake of assuming that you can afford to put less into such talks than you would if it was a big conference presentation. In particular, you will be asked questions that you may never have encountered before. This is partly because you will be speaking to people who have no preconceived notion that what they are about to ask is something that no one ever asks. You can either view this as refreshing or terrifying. Suddenly having to explain some of the most basic assumptions about your subject to smart, lateral thinkers can be a very challenging, but at the same time exhilarating, prospect. I suggest you relish it and remember, when answering questions, those magical words – "I don't know".

THE VENUE

Just as you need to know about your audience beforehand, you also need to know about the venue. This means more than knowing the address, although that in itself is fairly crucial. Ideally, you want to know the arrangement of the room and what audiovisual facilities are available. Is there a projector and screen, if you are planning to use slides? Do you need to bring your laptop? What sort of microphones will be in use, if any? How is the seating laid out? The answers to all these questions may impact upon the style and format of your talk and failing to have the answers may mean the difference between a perfunctory performance and a memorable lecture.

If it is the first time you have spoken at a particular venue make sure you arrive well before your lecture with enough time to check things out. Stand on the stage, try out the lectern and check how the slide advance works. See if there is a water glass and work out where you are going to sit or wait before the lecture starts or while you are being introduced.

If it is not possible to do this, perhaps because you are one of the speakers in a session that has already commenced, take the time to watch the other speakers. See how the stage is set up, watch what they are doing and anticipate any problems you might have by watching theirs.

ADVANCE MATERIALS

You may be required to provide the meeting organizers with details of your lecture in advance. This most commonly may take the form of an abstract or summary of your presentation.

When writing an abstract bear in mind the length – if they want 300 words don't give them 500 just because you happen to have a 500 word abstract on your desktop on a similar subject that you used last year and cannot be bothered updating and trimming it. Your abstract may be what tempts your audience in to hear you, especially if you are speaking at a conference with multiple parallel sessions. With this in mind make sure your abstract is clear, concise and if possible exciting.

At other times you may be required to submit a transcript of your lecture. Try, if at all possible to resist this. Generally it is not required – those organizers who ask for it are merely using it as a ruse to ensure you have actually prepared a lecture in advance. If you are forced to write down every word you are going to say it is enormously time-consuming, cumbersome and constraining when you actually come to deliver the lecture. Instead, offer the organizers a set of bullet points – perhaps as many as one for each slide you plan to use. This is much easier to prepare and will allow you greater flexibility on the day.

In a similar vein you will often be asked to provide your slides in advance. This is much commoner, especially if your talk is being sponsored by industry. For example, the rules and regulations by which pharmaceutical companies have to work vary throughout the world, but in most there is a requirement that any presentations made effectively in their name do not make outrageous claims for their products and do not disparage their competitors. These rules are perfectly reasonable, but they mean that the sponsor must have sight of your presentation for prior internal approval before you stand up. Some speakers are particularly precious about this and refuse to hand over their slides to sponsors in this way. In the past they may have got away with this, but no longer. If you wish to be a speaker at an industry sponsored event you either need to be prepared and willing to give your slides in advance or be replaced on the programme by someone who is.

The concern of some speakers to keep complete control of their slides, alluded to above, sometimes, however, does have a reasonable basis.

What if you have unpublished data on your slides or if you have borrowed slides from a colleague to whom you have expressly given your word that you will not pass them on to anyone else? Suddenly the idea of e-mailing them into the administrative void of a large company seems problematic. What to do? Well, the rules still stand and the company does need to see them, but they have no right to keep them and certainly no right to distribute them. This should be written into any contractual agreement you have with the company relating to the lecture.

Similar problems can arrive at the venue when your slides may need to be loaded onto a central computer. Again you are relinquishing control of your precious and, in some cases, your colleagues' precious slides. To get around this some speakers steadfastly refuse to hand over their slides and insist on delivering their lecture from their own laptop on the lectern. This, in my opinion, is ridiculous and more than often results in technical problems and significant distraction from the presentation.

Picture the scene: there are three speakers on the session programme. The first two have given their slides to the AV technician and their presentations go smoothly with seamless transition from one to the other. The third speaker, anxious about the fate of his slides goes up to the lectern carrying a laptop, trailing wires, and proceeds to start unplugging cables and even, in some cases, only at that point deciding to switch his computer on. All of this is happening under the increasingly irritated gaze of the audience who are starting to mutter comments along the lines of 'why couldn't he have done that before' and 'there's always one isn't there?' At this point the AV technician usually has to be called as there is some incompatibility. The laptop is of course a Mac and the speaker didn't mention this. Screen resolutions have to be adjusted and altogether it's a shambles. While there may not actually be audible slow hand-clapping it is easy for some of us to imagine it. Not the speaker though, for if he or she were the kind of lecturer who cared enough about the audience to consider this a possibility, it would never have occurred in the first place, for they would have properly prepared. Sometimes, of course, it is nothing short of an affectation. I am so important and my work so top secret that this is the only way I can give a lecture – so if you want me this is the way you get me – take it or leave it. If you are ever an organizer I suggest you leave it. These sorts of speaker are never the really big names – they are always the nearly big. No Nobel Laureate I have seen lecture has ever acted as if they were more important than the meeting – but that's often the way it is in life isn't it? The truly great are modest, humble even, and usually a pleasure to work with. It's the mediocre that induce chest pain.

HANDOUTS

Increasingly students in higher education expect handouts from lecturers. Other groups may also be looking for something tangible to use either during the lecture or as an *aide memoire* afterwards. Some lecturers steadfastly refuse to provide any form of handout stating that the audience should take their own notes. Others feel equally strongly that the lecturer's job is to ensure that the students or other members of the audience get the maximum out of attending the lecture and that one way of maximizing that experience is to provide a set of notes in the form of a handout.

Commonly these will be a list of key words or bulleted points, not unlike the content of the slides. In fact, many lecturers, me included, have given a simple paper printout out of the slide set as a handout. One advantage to this approach is that the students can use the paper slide set as a basis to take their own notes, supplementing what you have included in the slides with their own comments throughout the lecture. Generally, these are well received and of course are very easy to produce as you have already created the slide set.

There is one caveat however. If you have in your lecture some interesting points, questions or even jokes that rely on you showing one slide and then a follow up as the answer to the question or to deliver the punch line of the joke you may need to delete these from your handout otherwise your audience will be one step ahead of you.

Increasingly, handouts can be made available for download from a website. This saves time, money, trees and the inevitable confusion that the distribution of paper copies at the start of a lecture can cause.

BACK-UP

If you are using slides in your talk it is good to have a back up in case of disaster. If you have travelled to a meeting and are expecting the slides you e-mailed to the organizers the week before to be all ready and waiting at the AV technician's fingertips, think again. Of course they may be, but equally they may not. Take your presentation on your laptop and/or on a memory stick, or maybe even on three memory sticks just in case. It is also useful to have a paper print out copy of your slides. This can be used to check a few last minutes details or to make any notes that occur to you.

LIGHTING

It never ceases to amaze me that rooms that purport to be lecture theatres have lighting that is uncontrollable beyond the alternatives of 'on' and 'off'. As a speaker you should have control of the lighting. Ideally you do not want to stand up and sit down or answer questions from the floor in the dark. Equally you do not want to give your slide presentation in the full glare of banks of strip lighting that would put a solarium to shame. Nor do you want to give your talk in total blackout with only the slides illuminating the room. Blackout makes audiences uncomfortable, and of course they cannot see to make notes. If we ignore the artificial lighting, the same problem can occur with natural lighting. White painted lecture rooms with no blinds and a sunny day are the worst of all. I once turned up at the venue to prepare for my talk later that morning to discover the meeting was being held in a marquee on the expansive lawn of an old house - charming, but completely impractical. A marquee on a sunny day, even a moderately bright day, is no place to give a slide show. There was no way to reduce the glare within the tent and it was quickly apparent that none of us, neither the audience nor the speaker, could see the slides.

Ideally you want some happy medium – a room with controllable lighting, either through blinds that work or artificial lighting that can be differentially controlled – ideally off at the front of the room nearest the screen and on at the back. But, of course, you may not have any control over this. Always assume the worst and make sure that your slides are created with this possibility in mind. Make sure the contrast between text and background is pronounced and avoid images such as low resolution photographs that require blackout in order to be seen clearly. For more information on good slide design see Chapter 6.

WHERE TO STAND

Most of us give lectures standing on some form of stage or dais behind a lectern either to the right or left of the screen facing the audience. That's the convention, but it's not the only way to do it, and sometimes not the best.

Consider the issue of lecterns. In many cases you will have a choice of being lectern bound or to be roving. This has consequences for how you may be miked and how you may control your slides. In general, I would say that movement enhances a presentation and allows the lecturer to engage much more with their audience.

Lecterns do, however, present a comfort zone. You can have notes on them, you can grip their sides – tightly, with whitening knuckles – in order to avoid your hands shaking and you can hide half your trembling body behind one. But, if you are tempted to hide behind the lectern remember that a lecture is more that just your voice plus your slides. It is also an opportunity for one individual, in a short space of time, to share their knowledge and experience, and to teach the audience something new. To do so effectively requires all the communication skills you can muster and this includes your hands, your arms and your whole body. By moving around the stage you can add interest and emphasis, you can directly involve the audience and communicate more effectively.

And, what of leaving the stage altogether? In theatre they talk of the fourth wall – that invisible barrier through which we view the stage and its actions. Breaking the fourth wall is for many dramatists anathema, for others it is a device used sparingly, while for others it is standard fare. How should lecturers view this? We also have a fourth wall, but it's the easiest thing in the world to come down from that stage breaking through the wall and to wander among your audience. Now it has to be said that this technique is not for everyone, nor indeed every audience. Some speakers could never pull this off and many audiences find it acutely uncomfortable to become part of the show. However, some speakers do it marvellously, and their approach is one which enlivens their lectures and heightens the appreciation of their audiences. I have seen it fail and succeed with equally spectacular results. If you do chose to try this technique here are some tips:

- This approach works best with smaller audiences – I would say that 50 is the upper limit. The room layout is important. If the audience is in standard theatre style seating – i.e. in rows, the best you can do is go up and down the aisles, whereas if they are in a cabaret setting, i.e. seated at round tables of 6-10 then you can go from table to table.

- If you are going to wander about, are you going to interact with the audience, asking questions and making comments? If so, consider how their responses are going to be heard – do you have hand-held mikes at your disposal or will you simply have to repeat and relay their comments to the audience? Be careful with this approach that you don't turn into Jerry Springer, or your lecture may turn into his show – memorable for all the wrong reasons.

- Do it sparingly – if you are giving a series of lectures over a day to a single group, then using a mixture of wandering and more conventional lectern bound presentations may work best.

- Judge the mood of the audience – if they are edgy and made uncomfortable by your roving go back to the lectern. This is difficult to quantify, but you'll know it when you see it.

The most extreme form of moving from the stage is to give your lecture from the back of the room rather than the front. You might choose to do this because of the room layout – you can't see your own slides from the front or perhaps you can't control the slides from the front.

I have had to do this only twice and in neither case did it work. The audience can hear you, but not see you and you cannot see them, other than the backs of their heads. It is very difficult to judge reactions and interest levels from an audience's back, and I would not recommend this approach.

If you do choose to stand at the lectern beware of the glass or open lectern especially if you are a fiddler or a dancer. If nerves force you to wind one leg around the other so you end up standing like a constipated stork, remember you will be seen and such bird-like behaviour can be distracting even to the most attentive audience.

The title of this section was 'Where' not 'How' to stand, but we have strayed into the realm of deportment. Do try to stand up straight when speaking. I know I sound like your mother, but you will look better and more importantly you will sound better.

MICROPHONES

"Testing, testing, one, two, three." Yes, you may be miked up and be asked to check the levels like a proper rock star. Microphones will be the norm in a large lecture hall or conference setting, and a variety of different mikes might be used.

With hand-held mikes singers make it look so easy – but remember that most of them are miming. If you are using one keep it a fixed distance from your mouth and lock that position. If you turn your head to look at the screen the mike has to go too. This seems obvious, but just watch and listen to the inexperienced and you will get something like: "Good morning. In this first slide you can see - muffle muffle muffle, which I am sure you will agree is - muffle muffle muffle. This graph highlights the important point - muffle muffle muffle...." And so on. It can be really charming, but of course completely useless as a lecture.

The same applies to lectern mikes – if you move your head away from the lectern you cannot be heard. In this case, however, you can't move the mike- it's fixed – so you have to be more disciplined in your movements.

Freedom for roamers is provided by lapel mikes and head-set mikes. Either are fixed to you so whatever you choose to get up to, on or off the lectern, you should be audible. Just don't wander too near the loud speakers lest you deafen the audience with whining feedback.

LASER POINTERS

If you don't know how to turn it on and have to be helped by the chairman or the last speaker, don't use one. If your hands shake, don't use one. If you look at the screen and turn away from the audience, and the microphone, to use the pointer and forget to turn back again, don't use one. If you are a waver, pointing it all over the room like some crazed hit-man trying to identify a target, don't use one.

In short, unless you really feel comfortable try to get away from relying on a pointer. I know such advice is anathema to some speakers who feel they are enhancing every word they say by pointing at every detail of a slide. But the simple reality is that you're not. Laser pointing can be clumsy, distracting, misguided and just plain irritating. Better to design your slides so that they do not require you to point out specific sections of them.

One other practical point that should be remembered if you are giving a talk in a room where there is more than one screen, such as a large auditorium, pointing at one screen will not be visible on the others. Similarly, if your lecture is being video-conferenced your laser pointing will not be seen by the audience at the end of the line. In these latter cases if you must point then you will require access to the cursor, usually on the laptop. But again this can be very clumsy and I would recommend for simplicity's sake to steer clear of pointing. Your words and your slides should need no red dot or computer cursor to underline them.

SLIDE ADVANCE

Another reliable source of comic relief for the audience is the slide advance. These come in all sorts of shapes and sizes, and because of that speakers who have not taken the time to check beforehand invariably find themselves laser-pointing instead of changing the slides, or, if they have managed to identify the slide control on the lectern, reversing instead of advancing.

Occasionally at large meetings the slides will be controlled by the AV technician and you will have a "slide advance" controller that is not connected to the computer, but to a signal in the AV technician's box. When you press the button, they get a signal and advance the slide. All well and good until you want to go back or if you have accidently pressed your controller twice. In this case you will simply have to ask the technician to go to the slide you want. All of this can be especially disconcerting if the first time you encounter this system is when you are at the lectern giving your talk. Again, a little preparation can save a lot of panic.

BEING PHOTOGRAPHED

Particularly at large meetings when you get up and stand at the lectern to deliver your lecture you may find yourself not only facing the audience, but also a flash photographer. While you are doing your introduction you may be distracted by him or her wandering around at the foot of the stage flashing away. Often photographers are very single minded and all they are interested in is getting the right shots. This may entail a complete disregard for your lecture as he climbs on to the stage and starts flashing a few feet or, in some extreme cases, inches from your face. It is very difficult not to be put off by this behaviour, but you must try to ignore it. This is easier to do if you know it's going to happen and the best way to check this out is by watching the treatment of the speakers on the programme before you.

Sometimes it will not be an official photographer, but someone in the audience. This is not usually because they want to add you to their album, but because they are interested in your slides. These days, with improvements in camera equipment, people who want to do this can usually avoid using flashes and therefore it is much less distracting, but it will occasionally occur and you have to be unfazed. That said some lecturers find it intolerable. I remember attending a lecture given by the late Stephen Jay Gould who was adamant that he would not be photographed. During the talk a flash went off and he reprimanded the audience. When the flash went off again it nearly ended the lecture, for to make matters worse, the one taking the pictures was actually the chairman sitting in the front row.

BEING RECORDED OR FILMED

Increasingly lectures are being filmed or recorded. This may happen at universities so that a large class, which cannot be accommodated in the lecture theatre, may watch the lecture at a later date. It may also be used for archiving or for uploading on to websites or even for podcasting. Whatever the reason someone should have asked your permission beforehand. While you might not want to take them to court, it would be a common courtesy to seek your consent before being immortalised on video.

Personally, I do not like being filmed while lecturing. A lecture is a live event and a filmed lecture often appears stilted and odd when played back. Also I find the very act of being filmed alters the way I lecture, perhaps actually making me stilted and odd. Whatever the reasons, I think it is like watching the video of a stage play rather than the film adaptation. The play may have been spell-binding as a live performance, but the video of it is lacklustre.

Despite these caveats, if you are being filmed, ask for a copy – you never know when it might come in useful. Perhaps a potential commercial client will want to see some evidence of you in action, or perhaps you might want to use the footage on your website. Although these uses may strike you as unlikely there is also another, much better reason for asking for a copy. It will allow you to review your performance and to see yourself as others see you. Again I should emphasise that I do not believe a filmed lecture necessarily reflects your live performance, but it will allow you to see your more obvious traits – that annoying habit of picking at your ears or of playing with your hair, or your use of "ummh" as a vocal punctuation mark.

In many training courses for new lecturers, presenters or public speakers part of the training, indeed often its culmination, will be filming the presenter giving a short lecture and then going over it with them to critique it. If you have never done this I do recommend it. Even if you have done it before it is well worth a refresher. "Do I look like that?" "Do I *sound* like that?" "What *am* I doing with that laser pointer?" If someone is filming you anyway view it as a gift that will allow you to do your own review and critique, and perhaps, if you are feeling strong enough, to go over it with someone you trust.

DRESS CODES

What should you wear when you give a talk? There is, of course, no single answer to this. Even the quip "clothes" is not necessarily appropriate - for example, it may not be welcome if you happen to be giving a talk at a naturists' convention. In that situation, and in any other, it is best to think how your audience will be dressed and try to be a little more formal than them. In your lecture you are planning to expound on your chosen subject and to be authoritative. This will be difficult if you are in jeans and a t-shirt while everyone else is in black tie and evening gowns. If in doubt err on the more formal – you can always remove a jacket and tie, or roll up your blouse sleeves or slip off the tiara, but it is difficult to transform yourself in the opposite direction.

Ultimately what you are wearing should not be an issue and like good background music should be completely unnoticed by the audience, and by you. You should feel comfortable and they should find your attire unremarkable. I once attended a lecture where an American professor gave her talk in a sweater that had a dramatic picture of a tiger emblazoned across it. Whenever anyone referred to her presentation afterwards it was "the one given by the tiger lady." You do not want to be remembered that way.

WATER

Lecturers, especially nervous ones, get thirsty. The adrenaline dries your mouth and unless you have a drink you feel you will not be able to breathe effectively never mind speak. A water glass, however, can be a banana skin of the first order – so beware. A lot of lecterns are tilted at an angle sloping towards the speaker. I have often seen a speaker pick up a water glass from an adjacent (flat) surface, take a sip, and then put it down on the sloping lectern. The results are variable, but usually comical. This is especially disconcerting if comedy was not the desired effect at that point in the lecture. And somehow you don't really feel the same way about the lecturer again after they have spilled water over their laptop and their trousers and said a four letter word into the microphone more clearly than anything else they have said up until that point.

TOILETS

If you are going to drink water you have to consider the consequences. What advice can I give you on that score? Well, you're all grown up and I shouldn't really have to go into this, but suffice to say it's generally a better idea to go *before* rather than *during*.

This chapter has been about preparation and just about everything you need to think about apart from the actual lecture. Now we have to think about how to design and construct the lecture itself.

2

THE BEGINNING:

"BEST BEGUN IS HALF DONE"

How you begin your presentation is important. It is important because it sets the scene for what is to come, it allows you to connect with the audience and get them on your side and it allows you to take control and that's your job. Also, it is generally foolish to ignore the advice of Mary Poppins.

INTRODUCTIONS

In many meeting or conference settings you will be introduced by a chairman or chairwoman. In order to facilitate this, and to allow them to say a few words about you and your background, you may have been asked to provide a short biography. If asked to provide this, do so and preferably in advance, for then you can control what they are going to say about you and they will not be reliant on an out-of-date profile from an old website.

Keep it simple and short enough to avoid embarrassment for all concerned. If ever I am asked how I would like to be introduced I answer: "briefly". On occasion I have been introduced by chairmen who have done nothing short of reading out my entire CV – one even gave my date of birth, which I found surprisingly shocking, given that I am not particularly vain about age. Others have listed every honour ever received from higher degrees to cycling proficiency badges and created such a build up that when I stood up my first words were to thank them for their generous introduction and to state that now even I could not wait to hear what I was going to say.

GETTING THEIR ATTENTION

When you are introduced it is the chair's job to get the attention of the audience. In other settings, where there is no chair, you will have to introduce yourself and in such cases you will be responsible for getting their attention.

Polite groups will quieten down the moment you stand up and take your place; others may need a moment to pull themselves together; while some will need nothing short of a klaxon to bring them to order. You may need to use the lights in the room as an accomplice – dimming them produces the same effect as in the cinema – people stop chatting, sit back and wait for the main feature. Other ploys involve stating loudly and clearly your "Good Morning" while some lecturers will simply stand at the lectern and wait. For some audiences this works well, as a ripple of realization and embarrassment at their continued chatter sweeps across the room. When the decibels have sufficiently subsided you can begin and you have not even raised your voice. Youthful and more spirited audiences, such as some undergraduate groups, may need a firmer hand both before the lecture to get their attention and during the lecture to keep it. The latter will be discussed in Chapter 7.

However you choose to get the audience's attention it is an essential first step because the audience needs to know the lecture has started and only then can you get properly underway.

If introducing yourself do so briefly and if appropriate give your credentials, e.g.

> *My name is Joe Bloggs and I am Director of Marketing at Megacorps International*

or

> *I am Anna Smith and I have been studying the lifecycle of the bluebottle for the last three years as part of my PhD.*

This introduction can be usefully accompanied by a title slide that not only has the title of your lecture, but also your name and affiliations.

So, you are at the lectern, the audience knows your name, perhaps where you have come from and they are sufficiently quiet for you to continue. What next? Your first priority is to connect with the audience – they have heard your name, but they do not really know who you are yet, what you are and how this is all going to go. You may be nervous, but in a way so are they. They will be asking themselves the usual questions: are you going to be boring like the last guy; will you be asking questions throughout; will it all be over our heads?

You need to reassure your audience that everything is going to be fine – you want them to enjoy your lecture and learn – you need them to relax and you can do that by revealing your humanity and connecting with them.

ICE BREAKERS

If you can connect with your audience in the first 10 seconds, you are a very long way to giving a good presentation. I know this is a cliché, but like most clichés, it's true.

How might you achieve this connection? You might use humour – the opening gag or one liner can be very effective – unless you're not funny, and let's face it some of us just aren't. Alternatively, it might be the moderately personal insight that draws the audience to glimpse the human behind the lectern e.g.

> *Ladies and Gentlemen, it's a pleasure to be here – the last time I was in Edinburgh was to sit my Membership exam – I'm glad to be back under less stressful circumstances.*

The statistician Jerome Cornfield once began his lecture with the following words:

> *On being asked to talk on the principles of research, my first thought was to arise after the chairman's introduction, to say, 'Be careful', and sit down... That principles of research do in fact exist, or that there are persons qualified to expound on them, are not self-evident...*

It might be simply warmth – the speaker that begins with an enthusiastic smile looks as if they are going to be more fun to listen to than one who begins by blowing his nose and shouting, "first slide!"

Timing is important, of course, you only get that one chance to make a first impression – yes, another cliché. Don't let the audience's first glimpse of you be one of someone fiddling with wires, laser pointers, or slide controls while being whispered to by the chairman about how to go forward and how to go back. That first 10 seconds was your chance and you blew it – you should have sorted all that out before and used those first precious moments to your advantage.

TAKING THE LEAD

As a lecturer you are in a privileged and powerful position, even if you don't realise it, and even if it doesn't necessarily feel like it. You have the floor and your audience is waiting for you to lead them on some form of educational journey. So be that leader and take charge of the situation, but not in any overbearing way, but rather by engaging with your audience. The spirit should be more: we are in this together and this is the plan. Leadership is about authority, but it is also about compassion and inclusivity. Leaders are also the ones with the compass and the map.

Thus, leadership implies direction and after the preliminaries I believe it is crucial for the lecturer to state clearly the objectives of the talk, or in other words to say what you are going to say, and outline the talk.

OUTLINING THE TALK

There are several different ways to do this. At its simplest this may involve showing a single introductory slide with 3-5 points that you plan to cover in the course of your talk (figure 2.1). These bullet points may be the learning objectives for the lecture, i.e. what you are hoping each of the audience will know or be able to do by the end of your talk.

Alternatively, you may state your objectives in the form of questions that you plan to answer. This can be useful as it acknowledges that there are questions and that your lecture is going to provide answers rather than simply pose even more difficult questions. Finally, instead of going straight to a list of objectives or questions you might spend a short time giving some form of introductory story or case study that prompts a few questions that you can then define and go on to answer, or which lead you into stating your objectives.

Fig. 2.1 A simple example of an outline slide.

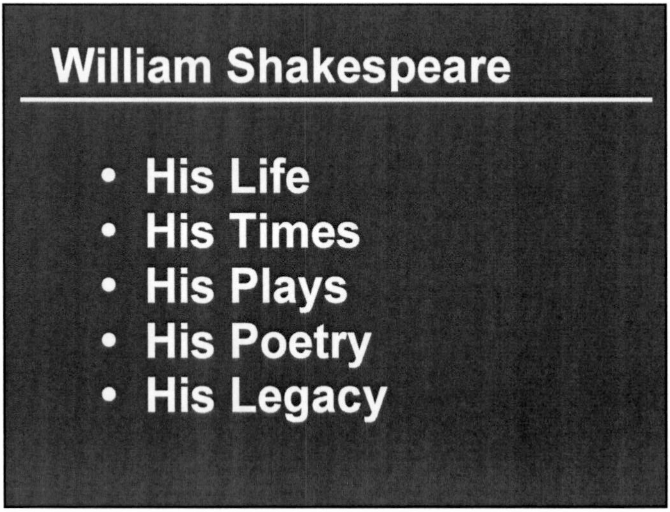

All these approaches assist the audience, but do mean that you as the lecturer have had to give some thought to the structure of your talk before actually standing up to deliver it. As discussed in the previous chapter the importance of this preparation cannot be underestimated. Some lecturers look as if they have just turned up and then effortlessly deliver a scintillating discourse of their subject that holds the audience in rapture. This is a fantasy; no one does that, at least not without a great deal of thought and preparation. The more effortless it looks, as with many practical skills, the harder the work that has gone into achieving that standard.

Although our task in hand is a little more challenging than tidying the nursery we have, as Mary Poppins requested, begun to the best of our ability and therefore may consider our job half done. The other half is what we are going to say next and how we are going to bring things to a conclusion. These are both dealt with in the following chapters.

3

THE MIDDLE:

JAM IN THE DOUGHNUT

Some people would argue that the middle of your talk is the least important part and all that it does is link the beginning and the end, both of which are more important and much more memorable.

In some ways this is true, and in some it is not. The beginning of your talk, as we discussed in Chapter 2, is undoubtedly important and needs to be carefully crafted to connect with your audience and to engage with them in the first 10 seconds.

Similarly, as we shall see in Chapter 4, the end of your talk is important because that is how you will be remembered. But, the middle is there to allow you expound on your subject, to give detail and example, to build arguments, to pose questions and to present convincing solutions.

Without the middle, your talk is nothing more than a few sound bites. Sound bites are what are remembered, but the middle, the meat of your talk, will be what determines if anyone thinks your sound bites worth remembering.

AIMS AND OBJECTIVES AND THEIR RELATIONSHIP

For any lecture, and certainly for any course of lectures that you teach, you should identify educational aims and objectives and be aware of the relationship between them. The aims are written as broad statement of overall purpose or intent, while the objectives are written as a set of desirable educational outcomes. Aims are therefore broad and general and objectives are narrow and specific. The best way to illustrate this is by using an example. The list of aims and associated objectives for a lecture I give on Clinical Trial Safety Reporting is shown below in table 3.1.

From this example it is clear that there are a small number of aims and a greater number of objectives. Each objective may be associated with a particular aim, and for each aim there are a number of related objectives. However, it may also be the case that an objective may be associated with more than one aim. For example, objective 2b - "Define a Serious Adverse Event (SAE)" – is a related objective of the second aim, but it could also have been listed as a related objective of the third aim. "To be able to assess a potential adverse event in a clinical trial subject" (Aim 2) it is necessary first to know what an adverse event is. But, equally, "To be able to report an adverse event appropriately" (Aim 3) it is also necessary to know the definition. There is, therefore, always a degree of overlap, which has not been taken into account in the table below. However, if the lecture aims and objectives are addressed in a linear fashion it may be assumed that, for example, before moving on to address aim 3, the objectives relating to aim 2 have been covered and may therefore be built upon rather than re-iterated.

Table 3.1. Example of Aims and Objectives for a Clinical Trial Safety Reporting lecture

Aims	Objectives
1. To understand the background to safety reporting in UK clinical trials.	a. Describe the legal framework for safety reporting in UK clinical trials. b. List the relevant UK laws c. Name the legal body responsible for oversight of this area. d. Describe the role and responsibilities of the sponsor in relation to safety reporting within UK clinical trials. e. Describe the role and responsibilities of the investigator in relation to safety reporting within UK clinical trials. f. Appreciate your legal responsibilities in this area.
2. To be able to assess a potential adverse event in a clinical trial subject.	a. Define an Adverse Event (AE). b. Define a Serious Adverse Event (SAE). c. Define a Suspected Unexpected Serious Adverse Reaction (SUSAR). d. Understand the term "causality" and give an example demonstrating its meaning. e. Understand the term "seriousness" and give an example demonstrating its meaning. f. Understand the term "expectedness" and give an example demonstrating its meaning.
3. To be able to report an adverse event appropriately.	a. Recognise an AE, SAE, and SUSAR within short clinical cases. b. Summarise the important relevant clinical information relating to an SAE for reporting purposes.

The objectives, as written, very much describe the educational product – in other words what I expect the student to be able to know, or be able to do, or what attitude they should have by the end of the lecture. Often these are referred to as addressing different domains –cognitive, psychomotor (skills) and attitudinal respectively.

Working out your aims and objectives of any lecture is not only essential to help design the presentation, but will also define the assessment used. Assessment tools in education are beyond the scope of the present book, but if you are a lecturer you will often find yourself involved in the assessment and evaluation of students. In the lecture set out in table 3.1 the objectives mainly relate to basic factual knowledge, understanding and practical aspects of being able to use a reporting system. The appropriate assessment of students at the end of this lecture would therefore include assessment of all three aspects. Objectives covering the attitudinal domain are generally more difficult to assess than those of the cognitive and skills domains, but if they are listed objectives they should also figure in the assessment process.

Remember, for objectives to be meaningful guides for the student and teacher they should be clear and specific. Terms such as "understand" are open to varied interpretation. I have attempted to address this in, for example, objectives 2d-f, where I have included in the objectives not simply an expectation of understanding, but a statement of how this understanding might be assessed. I have included the proviso that the student should "be able to give an example demonstrating its meaning".

The brief description above of aims and objectives does not do justice to this key part of educational theory and is presented either as a brief reminder to those who already know about it, or as a taster for those new to it. If you would like to explore this area further I would recommend one of the texts listed in the further reading appendix at the end of this book.

SIGNPOSTING THE WAY

If you have taken the time to define and state your objectives at the beginning of your lecture it takes very little further effort to order and organize your talk around them. As you proceed it is also highly desirable to offer your audience signposts along the way. This simply means either saying something or showing a slide to announce: now we are going to look at the first point or my second objective or our third question.

Signposting can be very effectively done using simple slides. A common and highly efficient technique is to show your objectives or questions as a short list of bullet points at the beginning and to repeat this slide each time you are embarking on a discussion of the next point. The same slide can be used as your summary slide at the end of the talk. The beauty of this approach is that the audience knows exactly where it is on the journey through your lecture. "She's going to cover four points and, OK, this is the second of them." A further subtlety that works well is to highlight on the slide which point or question you are addressing. This means rather than simply using the same slide each time, you use a version where all the points except the one you are introducing are dimmed or rendered a different colour. An example of this is shown in figure 3.1.

Signposting can also be a simple verbal technique. You will find that you do this naturally all the time. Words such as, "Well, now let's look at the three main causes for this recession", "Let's leave that aspect of Picasso's work and look at the next", "We've dealt with the internal causes of the rise of Fascism, let's now look at the external ones." It is a normal aspect of speech, and in particular argument, to lead your listener along. When you are lecturing you simply have to be a little more conscious of this, for the topic you will be speaking about, and the arguments associated with it, may be

FIG. 3.1 Examples of signposting slides.

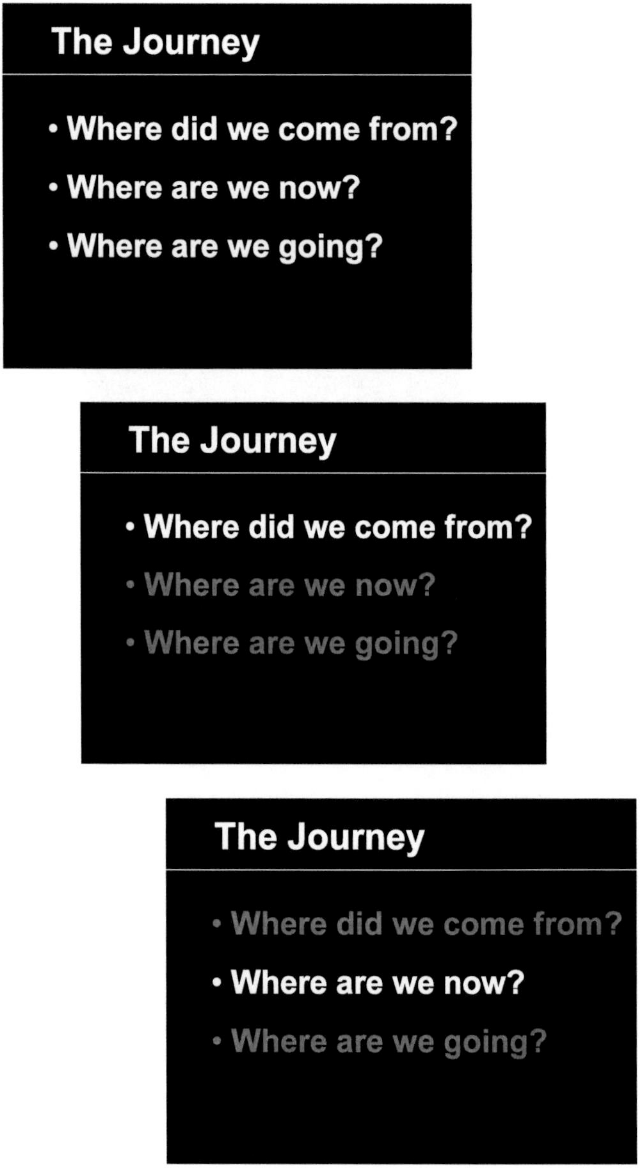

complex and will almost certainly be relatively unfamiliar to your audience.

DEVELOPMENT OF ARGUMENTS

I have alluded several times above to the development of arguments in your lecture. Unless you are lecturing on philosophy or legal reasoning you may think that this is not what your talks will be about. I would suggest otherwise.

No matter what you are talking about you are trying to impart knowledge. Knowledge is not just about facts, which are relatively easy to convey, but more about understanding. In order for your audience to understand what you are talking about you have to develop new ideas and concepts within which they can fit the facts. This makes the facts useful and useable. It also makes you a teacher. You must not assume that your audience understands your subject the way that you do; nor must you assume that they grasp its relevance or its importance. It is up to you to convince them, and that you must do through the use of carefully constructed argument.

CASE STUDIES

While much of what you include in your lecture may be of a theoretical nature, it is important to aid the learning of your audience through the use of concrete examples. In many instances this may be achieved through the use of case studies. This approach immediately brings the ideas and concepts you have been explaining to life. One course I teach concerns the legal framework surrounding the conduct of clinical research in the UK. This subject can be as dry as dust, but is of paramount importance to my audiences, which usually comprise clinical researchers from various professional groups. My job in those lectures is to tell them the facts about the law, but just as importantly it is also to make them see the relevance of these facts to their everyday work. I have to do this through a process of argument supplemented by a series of examples and case studies that transform the subject from one of merely academic interest to one that is real and very much alive.

LECTURE LENGTH

Every talk has to have a beginning and an end. Whether it has a middle of any substance depends on how long you have to speak. If you are to speak for more than five minutes you need some jam in the doughnut. If it's to be a standard 45 minute lecture you need a whole pot.

Some lecturers have a very elastic attitude to timing and unfortunately rather than being an insignificant problem this may become all that anyone remembers about their talk. Lecturers who consistently run over are, in my experience, rarely asked back. How do you pace your talk and ensure that you keep to your allotted time? If you prepare your lecture – using slides and perhaps note cards – you will be able to run through it beforehand in front of the mirror and time yourself. That would be a counsel of perfection, but people rarely do this and often prefer to wing it on the day. The next best thing would be to ensure that you have an appropriate number of slides. This varies from discipline to discipline because different professional groups use slides in different ways. A general rule of thumb is one slide for each minute of your talk and that includes your title slide and any closing acknowledgement slide. You should never have any more than one slide per minute and often you will need less. For example, an art history lecture may spend 45 minutes discussing two paintings and will use two slides which are studied and discussed in detail. If you stick to the one slide per minute rule you will be able to control the timing of your talk fairly well, but only if the slides you are using are simple and uncluttered, i.e. if they do not require you to spend more than one minute on each on them. You can find a simple set of rules to follow for the design of such slides set out in Chapter 6.

If you are not using any slides and you have chosen to write out your presentation, again it would be a very good idea to rehearse it beforehand to judge the timing. Another useful rule of thumb here is that a normal speaking pace for a lecture should be about 150 words per minute. What does that feel like? Because of nerves most people have a tendency to speak too quickly when they are lecturing. To counteract this you should try to speak in a way that sounds to you just a little unnaturally slow. If you do this what comes out sounds normal.

USING NOTES

If you are new to lecturing the thought of standing there for 45 minutes speaking seems overwhelming and you will automatically reach for a pen and paper to start drafting out your talk. You may be tempted to write the full lecture out in prose. Quickly you will find this very tedious as it is surprising just how much you can say in 45 minutes and how time consuming it is to write it all down. Also you have to ask yourself how you will use such a transcript. Will you stand at the lectern and read it out. A lectern is quite literally where you read something and a lecture is quite literally a reading. Certainly in the past that was the way it was done – the lecturer, who was the only one who had access to the book, read portions of it out to his eager students. Nowadays students of all kinds expect more. They expect information, but also analysis, prioritization, examples and summaries. Yes, you could write it all down and read it out, but what was the point of standing there – why not just leave a pile of photocopies on the front desk and save your breath?

Although the temptation to go down this route is strong it should be resisted. If you need notes make them simply that

– notes. Don't use paper for one thing – it's too tempting to fill a whole page, and it's difficult to find your way through a dense piece of writing on A4 sheets when you are nervous at a lectern. Rather, use index cards and perhaps have one for each of the slides you plan to show. On the cards have some simple key words or bullet points that will prompt you. Of course your slides, if they have been well designed using the simple rules outlined in Chapter 6, will also consist of key words and bullet points, so perhaps you could use these instead of your cards.

Some lecturers never want to relinquish their notes, but when you find the confidence to do so you will enjoy a new found sense of freedom coupled with a renewed ability to attend to your audience and to think about *how* you are giving your talk rather than simply its contents.

TONE OF VOICE AND BODY LANGUAGE

What you say is only one aspect of how you communicate. Your audience will also garner a lot of information from how you say it - your tone - and from non-verbal forms of communication or body language. If you are listening to a lecturer who is speaking a language you do not understand you are still likely to make decisions about the quality of the presentation. For example, warmth, enthusiasm and trust are communicated largely through the lecturer's tone and body language. How we stand or sit, how we walk, how we gesture, our facial expressions, even what we do with our feet can convey a great deal of information and often reveals our attitudes and feelings.

The trick is to be aware of these forms of communication and to use them to your advantage.

To ensure your tone is conducive to effective lecturing you should pay attention to the speed and volume of your voice as well as its rhythm and pauses. Try to avoid a monotonous drone; instead make your voice interesting by varying the pace of your speech and using stresses to emphasise points. Listen to radio news readers to get some tips on how to do this and don't forget to breathe, for your voice is, after all, nothing more than air.

Some of your body language will be so ingrained and subconscious that it will be difficult to control, but some aspects can be adjusted. Smile and adopt an open rather than a closed posture, by not folding your arms or crossing your legs. Try to maintain eye contact with different members of the audience and never turn your back on them.

Of course body language is a dialogue, and as well as speaking to your audience without words, they will also be speaking to you. If you can read them, the signs are there and can be useful. As you are lecturing it is important to know if you are hitting the right mark with your audience. Are you being understood or is what you are saying going over their heads? Do they agree with you? Have you perplexed them with one of your arguments? Or could you simply be boring them? If you look at members of your audience you will be able to read the tell-tale signs of all these feelings.

For example, if there is good eye contact and there are nodding heads as you present your arguments, these actions are likely to signify that you are being followed. On the other hand, if all you can see are the tops of people's heads and if there is audible shuffling in the room you may have a problem. If people are starting to close up – folding their arms, leaning backwards, crossing their legs and holding their notes up in front of them as a barrier between them and you, then you may have to re-engage with the audience, unless of course it is too late and you have lost them for good. In these circumstances it may be useful to pause and recap, even if it means turning off the slides and raising the lights for a minute or two. It may also require you to change tack in the middle of your lecture. This is difficult to do unless you are well-practiced, but it might save the lecture. You might also want to engage with the audience and ask them direct questions: "I always find this concept quite challenging – would you like me to go over it again?" or "Tell me – is this making sense to you?"

The middle of your lecture is its substance and is usually where the hard work has to be put in. The captivating opening and the big finish can be show without real depth, but the middle cannot. In this chapter I have emphasised the importance of planning, using aims and objectives to chart the presentation and the use of various devices to signpost the way for your listeners. As with every aspect of effective lecturing, preparation is the key, coupled with consideration for your audience.

4

THE END:

LEAVING A GOOD TASTE IN THEIR MOUTHS

The ice is well and truly broken; the audience has been led by the hand through a well signposted presentation and now comes the time to tie things up.

KNOWING WHEN TO STOP

When asked how you should end a lecture, my usual answer is, "on time". That is the basic prerequisite of a good lecture as running over irritates audiences and can throw a programme, on which you are only one of the speakers, into disarray. Professionals keep to time. They do so, however, unobtrusively. You should not have to consult your pocket watch or strain to see the wall clock. Instead you should be quietly aware of the time, and because you have prepared your lecture well and have run through it to check timings you will be aware of approximately how long you should take. And, there's the audience to guide you too. When the shuffling starts or when the stomachs start to rumble you know time is running out; when the audience actually start to leave you know that it's up. Also, remember the words of the English Judge Lord Birkett:

> *I do not object to people looking at their watches when I am speaking. But I strongly object when they start shaking them to make certain they are still going.*

KNOWING HOW TO STOP

Don't simply stop speaking and expect your audience to know it's over. If your talk simple fizzles out in this way and no one in the room is sure whether it is over or not, it creates a tension that is unnecessary and easily avoided. Think how it works in the cinema or the theatre. *The End* appears, or the curtain falls, or the stage lights dim. You will not have ready access to a curtain or complex stage lighting, but some lecturers do favour a final slide which is the equivalent of the cinematic *The End*. I have seen sunsets as well as gravestones and even photos of generous backsides all used to signify the end. In general, I would counsel against the use of such gimmicks, as they are rather clichéd and if you give it some thought you can probably do better.

Assuming your timing is under control, what then is the best way to draw proceedings to a close? Again simplicity should reign. The classic lecturing mantra – say what you're going to say; say it: and then say what you've said - guides the way. Saying what you've said usually translates into summarizing your talk. Ideally this can be done in a single slide with 3-5 bullet points. This allows you to recap the main learning points you had identified and hoped to convey in your lecture.

An example of such a summary slide is shown in figure 4.1. As always with any text slide limit the number of lines of text to 5-7 and remember to include the title line in that count. An example of a summary slide to avoid is shown in figure 4.2.

Fig. 4.1 An example of a good summary slide

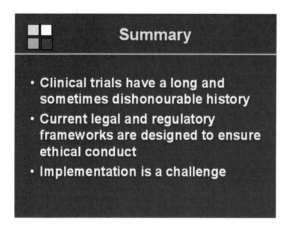

Fig. 4.2 An example of a not so good summary slide

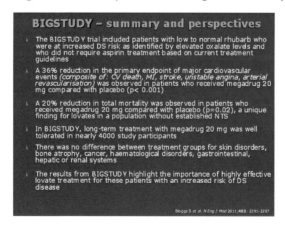

An alternative approach to the standard summary slide which works well is using the same signpost slide that you began with, thus topping and tailing the lecture with the same list of objectives (See Chapter 3 Signposting and figure 3.1). In this way you can recap in your own words while the list of objectives is back on the screen.

You could end the lecture, with the customary, "Ladies and Gentlemen, thank you for your attention" because just as it is important to signpost the lecture throughout, it is also important to let your audience know when it is over by displaying a visual or verbal STOP sign – i.e. the lecture is now over and you can applaud and/or leave.

Alternatively, you may wish to mirror your opening and finish on a lighter note. This can take various forms. Often lecturers will employ a relevant and perhaps pithy or humorous quotation that sums up what the lecture has all been about. For example, in speaking about lifestyle changes and the prevention of heart disease I have used some immortal words of the American author, Mark Twain:

> *A habit cannot be tossed out the window; it must be coaxed down the stairs a step at a time.*

Perhaps if you are more of a visual person, you may wish to use a cartoon or a photograph that again is relevant to the subject and thrust of the talk, but which may raise a laugh and relax the audience into warmer applause.

Lastly, you could show a short video clip. The internet abounds with these and they are easily inserted as MPEGs into your PowerPoint presentation. Television adverts from around the world often work well. They are short – usually about 30 seconds – and often the humour is visual and universal. You will find an abundance of these if you look for them on the internet and it is best to use foreign ads as your audience is then less likely to have seen them before. Do be careful, though, for while they are all funny some are simply silly and others may be offensive.

Like quotations and pictures, however, these only work if they are relevant to the lecture's content. Don't be tempted to include something you found that you thought was hysterical unless you can convince yourself that it has a place in the lecture. If you are stylistically tone deaf in this regard and cannot judge for yourself, ask someone who you trust to guide you. Remember the only thing worse than no one laughing at your jokes is one person laughing – you. Try not to laugh too heartily at your own jokes. In fact try to tell jokes and show funnies with as straight a face as you can – it will be better and the joke will have a greater impact.

Ending on a high note is desirable for the audience may leave remembering how much they enjoyed your lecture based on the last few minutes of the talk. Indeed, when we consider the way our attention works you can assume that your audience was awake at the beginning of your talk, and depending on the length for a portion or portions of the middle interspersed with a series of micro-sleeps, and that they may only reawaken for your big finish.

From an educational point of view a recap of the main points reinforced by a strong final message, whether it is in the form of a quotation, a picture or a video will help the audience achieve the learning objectives you have defined.

5

DEALING WITH QUESTIONS:

NO SUCH THING AS A STUPID ANSWER?

Many lectures will be followed by some form of question and answer or Q&A session. This may be informal, with some of the audience coming up to speak to you at the end, or it may be a formal chair led activity that has been carefully timetabled.

Many speakers have little problem or nervousness about giving a lecture, but become stressed when faced with the questions from an audience. The reasons for this are simple. Your lecture can be prepared and rehearsed and you are in control. When the questions come you are no longer in control, you are in uncharted territory and because you may be asked anything how can you prepare, and how can you expect to survive with your professional reputation intact?

Well, of course that's not really the way it will be. After all, you have been asked to give the talk in the first place because you know something about the topic. Indeed, you may be talking about your own work in which case who is there, not just in the audience but anywhere, who knows more about it than you? If you are reviewing a topic, again you will be in command of your material. If you have prepared the lecture and, in doing so, answered your own queries to your personal satisfaction, chances are that you will have anticipated most of the questions that your audience might pose. So don't panic. Listen to the question –that might seem obvious, but it's not always – then answer it to the best of your ability. If possible draw on your experience: "In our lab we have had most success with this particular cell line"; "In practice I have found that supplier to be the most reliable."

WHEN YOU DON'T KNOW THE ANSWER

If this were a book about media training or how to behave in court I might be giving advice about how not to answer the question or how never to answer more than what was asked, but this is an educational setting. A questioner has been brave enough to put their hand up and ask a question: they deserve an answer. They also deserve a straight answer and that might be, "I don't know". If you've never tried that answer, give it a go and you may be surprised by the results. Most lecturers shy away from admitting they do not know the answer to a question and turn it around so they end up answering another question that they can answer. But, an audience has a collective bullshit detector and this approach will mark you out as a fake. If you say "I don't know" perhaps followed up by "but, it's an important question and I will try to find that out for you – perhaps you could give me your contact details at the end" you will be surprised just how refreshing people will find it, and how much more impressive you will be as a speaker.

There may also be the opportunity, depending on the setting, to enter into a dialogue. "That's an interesting question – what do you think", or "Let's see what the audience thinks – with a show of hands how many agree that Anna Karenina is Tolstoy's greatest work." This approach may turn your Q&A into a more interactive teaching session, but if there's time this will probably be more useful to the audience than anything else you could do. People attending a lecture often say that they learn more from the Q&A than they do from the lecture itself. Depending on the quality of the lecture this can certainly be true, but it also reveals something about the way many of us learn. Rather than simply being on the receiving end of a barrage of facts, we may get much more out of a more Socratic method of teaching where the student is guided through an argument by the back and forth exchange of pertinent questions and answers which serve to illuminate the topic. In some ways this approach does not readily lend itself to the standard lecture format. Despite this difficulty you may still be able to sample this technique. For example, you might construct your lecture around a series of questions for which you provide the answers. Also you may stop at various points in your talk and pose questions directly to your audience. But, perhaps the most obvious place for this technique is in the Q&A session.

Of course for this to work you need to have the confidence to facilitate it and deal with the possible silences that might ensue, as well as the ability to ensure that the session is not hijacked by one or two more outspoken members of the audience. Facilitation comprises a different, but related, set of skills to lecturing and much has been written about it. When lecturing, you may be called upon to employ a varied set of additional techniques, particularly if you are addressing a small group. A detailed discussion of these skills and techniques is beyond the scope of this book, but you can find some useful and relevant further reading in the appendix at the end.

PANEL DISCUSSIONS

If you are speaking at a meeting it may be organized in such a way that instead of taking questions at the end of each lecture, there is a combined Q&A with all the speakers from the session invited back up on to the stage to share the questions. Such a session will usually be facilitated by a chairman or woman, and questions from the audience will be directed, as appropriate, at each speaker. Often a question once answered will be opened to the rest of the panel for comment.

Resist the temptation, however strong, to violently disagree with your co-speakers, even if what they have said is nonsense. This does not mean you shouldn't say what you think, but do it in a civilized and always polite way. "While my colleague makes a good point I do think that the public execution of all cabinet ministers may be a step too far at this point. Perhaps public censure should be our first approach." Sometimes your co-speakers will not be as well brought up as you, and may become personal or just downright rude. Do not sink to their level. Keep your composure and keep smiling; the audience will see what is happening. If you stay calm, retain your dignity and exhibit "grace under pressure" you will be the model of courage as defined by Ernest Hemingway, and a model of authority appreciated by your audience and the chair. Always let the ranting of others, whether it be from your co-speakers or from one of the audience on the floor, say more about them than about you. Above all do not rise to the bait - just let your co-speakers knock themselves out.

One more point about panel discussions - often the panel will be photographed. If you have a choice of seats when you join the panel sit on the far right facing the audience – then when you are photographed or viewed from the front you will be the first noticed or mentioned in a caption under the photograph– except of course in the Arabic and Hebrew speaking world where the opposite will be true.

TYPES OF QUESTION

The audience may pose questions by different methods. Simplest of all is when one of the audience puts up their hand and asks. This may happen during the lecture or afterwards. Some lecturers like to draw a clear dividing line between their lecture and the questions and do not like to be interrupted with premature questions from the floor. If this is the case, it is worth informing your audience of this as part of your introduction, but make sure you do it politely, at the same time reassuring them that there will be time to take questions at the end.

Questions may also be written down on cards and handed either directly to the speaker, or the chair, at the end of the lecture. This is common practice at large meetings, particularly where the audience's first language is not the same as the speaker's. Because there will usually be a fixed time allotted to questions only a portion of the questions, either asked directly or through cards, can be answered. If there are a large number of questions it is important that your answers are brief and to the point. Otherwise, you may use up all your time long-windedly answering a single question.

Beware the questioner who begins: "Thank you for that lecture: I have three questions." At this point I usually intercede and request that they ask them one at a time, otherwise we inevitably end up playing the game a few sentences later of: "And what was the third question again?"

This just avoids wasting time repeating things, and ensures that you maintain your control of the session.

As mentioned earlier, this feeling of control is very important for most lecturers and the Q&A may jeopardise it. They may have been in charge during the actual lecture, but now that they are standing there naked and facing the lions, the idea of control is a distant memory. This, however, need not be the case. At the end of your talk your chair will either open up the session to questions or, in the absence of a chair, you may have to do this yourself. "Thank you for your attention – I would now be happy to try and answer any questions you may have." Note the use of the word "try". Immediately you acknowledge that a fool can ask more questions than a wise man can answer. You are not superman and you certainly do not know everything. But, you are emphasising that you will do your best.

Be aware that questions are often posed that have little to do with your lecture, and more to do with your general area of expertise. Remember, you were introduced with some credentials for giving the lecture in the first place, and the audience is aware of your background, so be prepared for some left-field questions, as well as those about the content of your lecture. Although I say "be prepared" I don't of course mean crib up on a variety of answers – you can't do that, because you don't know what you might be asked. But, you can have your game face on and try not to look too astonished, dismayed, terrified or otherwise flummoxed when someone asks you about what you think of the article in the Daily Post that morning, which says all lecturers are simply people that cannot 'do' so they have to 'teach'.

If hands do not go up at your invitation to ask questions, do not panic, or at least do not look as if you are panicking. Simply ask again in a gently encouraging manner and perhaps make a joke: "Well, either I must be getting better at this, or you must be smarter than my usual audience– usually I have to explain it all at least twice for people to get it." You might also try to get the questions going by posing one yourself: "I'm often asked how this applies to the study of Italian neo-realist cinema – let me expand on that…" If there are still no hands, and perhaps no laughs, it's done and time to make a dignified exit. "Well, if there are no questions let me thank you once again for coming along."

Sometimes, especially in larger audiences, there will be people who have a burning question but who are too shy to ask it from the floor. To accommodate these people it is good practice to linger visibly at the front of the room while the audience is leaving in order to give them a chance to approach you and ask their question in person. You may say why would I waste my time doing that? – I'm busy; I've got places to go. Well, if you are a lecturer who wants to give an effective presentation you need to think about your audience. Part of that is being considerate enough to give those who are interested, but shy, access to your important, busy mind. But, this can be a two-way process for by listening carefully to the questions you are asked you might decide that you have to change your approach. If you are consistently asked to clarify a point in one of your arguments then perhaps it is time to adjust the way you make that point in the lecture next time.

TYPES OF QUESTIONER

Several types of people ask questions. There are those who simply want some further information or clarification of a point. This is straightforward and, perhaps if you are new to lecturing, you might expect this to be the one and only category of questioner. It will be the most common reason behind a question but, unfortunately, some people who raise their hand have a different agenda as illustrated below.

First, you might be quizzed by someone who already knows the answer to the question they are asking, but is more interested in showing off to the room that they have asked it. This might be a cocky, and usually junior, department member who is grandstanding for his senior colleagues, or it may be someone who is just a show-off by nature. Often, not only will they know the answer but they will also, given half a chance, answer it as well. "Thank you for your lecture. My question relates to the use of the term metaphysical in describing the poetry of Andrew Marvell. What is your position? I tend to concur with Professor Black on the subject but even he, I feel missed one of the key points which was..." Well, you might as well not be there. At this point if the Chair does not intervene to shut it down, or in their absence, you should politely interrupt, acknowledge the importance of the point and suggest "in the interests of time and because there are some other questions" that you move on. "Yes, the lady with the purple hat –you had a question?"

Second, is the wildcard questioner – the person you didn't know was in the room and when he or she asks a question you suddenly regret what you said earlier. This may be the recognized world expert on the subject that you have just tried to distil into a 25 minute presentation, or worse the author of the paper or book that you have just spent the last half hour refuting. This sometimes happens at large conferences and can be acutely uncomfortable for the speaker and gloriously entertaining for the rest of the audience. This is certainly one very good reason why it is never a good idea to be openly disparaging of other people's work, for unbeknownst to you they may be sitting in row 4 on the aisle and they might well have a concealed weapon.

And, last is the aggressive questioner – although sometimes there is no actual question to contend with just a tirade of abuse. "I think it is an outrage Dr Gaw that you have been allowed to speak at this conference"; "How dare you come here and talk about your so-called research when we all know you and folk like you are nothing but paid lackeys of the drug companies." I have been on the receiving end of both of these and the people who said them did look slightly crazed and as if they probably wrote angry letters to newspapers in green ink. In both cases I did not have to say anything as my audience took up my cause for me. My job, and yours if you are ever in a similar position, was simply to remain composed, to smile reassuringly, and to acknowledge their right to have their say and, in so doing, to be abusive, pompous and ill-informed all at the same time.

FOUR KEY STEPS TO ANSWERING QUESTIONS

1. Listen to the question

Rather obvious I know, but you will be surprised how much this helps. If you do not understand the question, perhaps because you cannot hear it properly, it involves terminology you don't understand or is being asked with a heavy accent, ask for clarification. You can do this simply by giving the question back in your own words. For example, "I'm sorry, I'm not quite sure what you mean – are you asking what *I* think of Napoleon's Russian campaign of 1812?" Hopefully this will illicit a simple "Yes" or perhaps a clearer question and you can then go on to answer it.

2. Answer the question that was asked

Generally it is a good idea only to answer what was asked of you and not to adopt the habit of a politician and answer only the question you really want to answer. I say that is generally the case, but there are instances when you may want to expand and you should certainly not ignore the actual question. Some Q&A sessions have a fixed time slot – say 10 minutes – and there may only be one raised hand in the room. If you do not think you are going to be asked anything else you could use the time usefully to reiterate your main points again. Do so by bridging from the question and your answer: "the answer to your question is no, I do not agree with Black's concerns about the origins of the galaxy, but he does raise some important points that were addressed by Green in his recent paper. A paper in which, as we saw, at the beginning of today's lecture he also talked about the origin of comets. It's very important to remember the three main points about comets…"

3. Don't make it up

So, you don't know the answer – say so. If you can't quite find it in you to do this, find a way to save face without resorting to making up an answer, because lying will be obvious to the audience. Delaying tactics may be usefully employed: "That's a good question on a number of levels and I'd like to think about it carefully before answering - perhaps we could have a discussion afterwards." If it's a fact that you have been asked that has either slipped your mind or that you never knew in the first place, a delaying tactic will not really work – it will be obvious that you either know it or you don't. Again don't make it up – instead make light of it and move on. "What was Mussorgsky's first name? Yes, as a Professor of the History of Russian Music I should really know that shouldn't I – sorry I think it must have been in the brain cell that died this morning."

4. Be gracious

I always try to put the audience at some ease by reminding them at the outset of the Q&A that there are no such things as stupid questions, with one possible exception. That is the question they ask themselves after the lecture when poring over their notes: "Why didn't I ask that at the time, when I had a chance?" Everything else is fair game. And all questions will be treated equally and with respect. I also remind them that no matter how silly they might feel not understanding something and having to ask about it, if they are wondering then there are likely to be others in the room in exactly the same boat.

While you may convince your audience that there is no such thing as a stupid question you might ponder a related question: Is there such a thing as a stupid answer? My answer would be an emphatic– yes. You can easily make a fool of your questioner by ridiculing their question. If you do this you deserve to be ridiculed in return, and you may be, by someone smarter than you – and yes, there is always someone else smarter than you in the room. Be gracious, i.e. do not be a smart ass. If anyone has been interested enough and brave enough to ask a question – no matter how simple, how obvious or how apparently naïve it seems – they deserve an answer, not approbation. Don't give stupid answers that reveal you to be an arrogant oaf.

6

USING SLIDES:

LESS IS MORE

Most lecturers will use visual aids to enhance, illustrate and signpost their presentations, and the most commonly used aid is the slide. Currently, slides will be almost universally produced using Microsoft PowerPoint although other similar software packages are available, such as Macintosh's Keynotes. In the past, most lecturers would have had to outsource the production of their slides to a graphics department, i.e. to a group of people who were trained and knew what they were doing. Now lecturers have the capacity to make their own slides, and as a consequence the quality of slides has diminished markedly in the last twenty years.

There are simple rules for making good slides, but most lecturers are either not aware of them, or do not feel they apply to them. I suspect it is the latter. The application of these rules generally results in simpler, cleaner, less cluttered slides, but many lecturers apparently see simplicity as something undesirable, preferring to present more rather than less, in case their lectures will be deemed simplistic and therefore insubstantial. In this respect the approach of the renowned architect Mies van der Rohe is appropriate – "Less is more" he counselled, and he was right.

As noted in the Introduction to this book keeping it simple is a highly desirable approach, and one that your audience will welcome. In this chapter I will outline the simple rules of slide design, which I have repackaged into a simple five step process. You can remember this approach using the following mnemonic – SWIPE. This stands for Style, Words, Images, Palette and Extras.

Before we elaborate on this it is worth acknowledging the subjective nature of this topic. For every pointer I offer there will be a lecturer who either disagrees with me or who thinks that my point is simply irrelevant. I would argue, however, that these rules are not about artistic niceties, but about whether your audience can see your slides, read them and assimilate your points quickly. Unless they can do this your lecture will not be enhanced by your slides and may even be destroyed by them. If you do follow these pointers you will produce slides that are clear, simple and that go a long way to enriching your lecture rather than diminishing it.

S IS FOR STYLE

The first thing you have to do when designing slides is to decide on their overall look, their format or, as I have termed it, their style. This includes choosing a background, deciding on the use of headers or other devices that will appear on every slide (such as your institution's logo), as well as the font or fonts used throughout. Different lecturers like different things –it would be boring if we were all the same, but within a lecture it is bad idea to try out every background and slide style in your library. The first rule when it comes to styling slides is consistency. Pick a style and stick with it throughout the lecture. Moreover, I would suggest that your style should be consistent between lectures as well as within them. This way your slides will be interchangeable between your lectures and it will be much easier to mix and match when making up a new talk.

The second rule in slide styling is simplicity. The array of different styles available as templates within the various software packages is bewildering. On top of that you have the ability to custom design your own, so the possibilities are literally limitless. Where do you begin? Again I would counsel a simple approach. Look at other lecturers' slides and decide what you like and what you think works well.

Several examples using templates available from PowerPoint are shown in figure 6.1. In my opinion all these have problems although I, like you, prefer some more than others.

Example (a) has clear simple text, but on a white background. Generally I, and many other presenters, prefer light text on a dark ground as it is easier to read and creates an illusion of depth in the slide. Also this example has a simple and colourful little logo that will be interesting for the first couple of slides but by slide 35 will have lost its appeal.

Example (b) has light text (white or yellow) on black, but again has that rather odd firework in the corner. Even if it's relevant to your talk it will become grating if it is present on every slide.

Example (c) has a background graphic which I feel adds unnecessary complexity to the slide and inevitably detracts from the texts and images. The font used is Times New

Roman, which is often thought to be more difficult to read on screen compared to Arial for example, even though it is easier to read in printed text. Also the colour scheme here is an odd brown and yellow combination, which to my eyes says "dull".

Example (d) is one I have seen used more than once, but my main concern here is why would you allocate a quarter of your precious slide space to a meaningless graphic that is again going to become very boring after a few slides.

These are just four templates selected from hundreds. Of course you can create and work to your own template, which can be anything you choose. Commonly this will be a plain simple monochromatic background with a simple header device and a simple uniform font. As noted above, I personally do not like meaningless graphics such as swirls or leaves or snippets of Mondrian's Art in the corners as I feel it detracts from the content of the slides and very quickly becomes boring.

The use of graduated backgrounds where the colour is darkest at the top or bottom of the slide and gradually lightens as you move down or up the slide can work well, but again it is a subtle complication that you don't really need so think carefully before you include it.

Some lecturers are fond of using background photographs which may or may not have anything to do with the content of the slide. An example is shown in figure 6.2. This is usually very distracting and should be avoided.

You may be obliged to have your institution's logo on the slide and indeed may be tied in to a corporate style overall. However, where possible keep these additional elements to a minimum especially when they include text. A University crest is one thing, but do you also need the full name of the college on every slide?

Fig 6.1 Examples of style templates for slides.

(a)

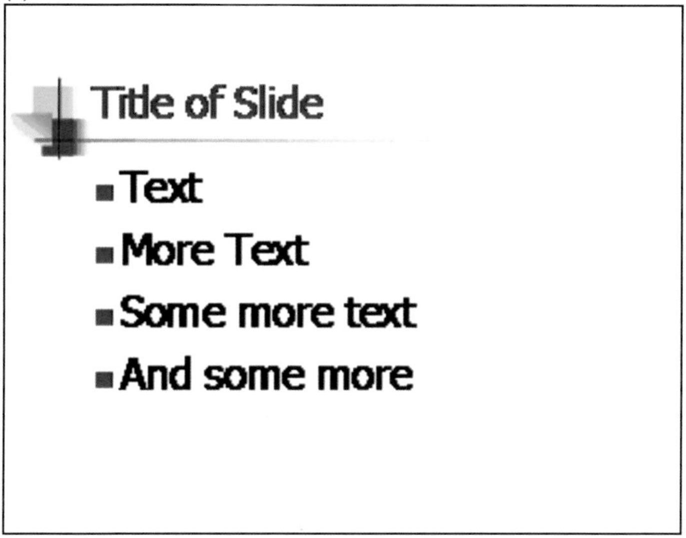

(b)

(c)

(d)

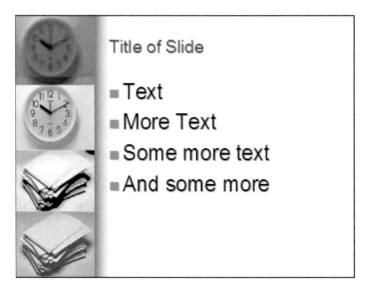

Fig. 6.2 Using a background photograph can be distracting.

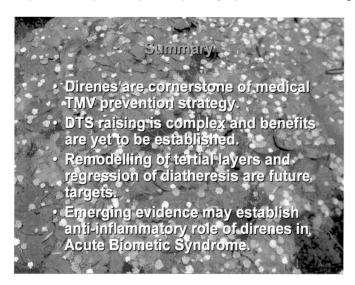

The criteria for choosing fonts are simple: the text must be clearly visible and easy to read. There are several *sans-serif* fonts, i.e. those without little twiddley bits around the letters. Examples of these are Arial, Verdana and Gill Sans MT. I find these fonts work very well. Again, as with backgrounds, consistency is important and the same font should be used throughout, although the size and /or colour may vary for emphasis and effect. When it comes to size, a useful guide is never to use a font size smaller than 24 – for example, the text sizes in figs 6.1 and 6.2 are 44 and 32 respectively.

W IS FOR WORDS

The most widely perpetrated slide crime is overuse of text. Virtually every guide that has ever been written on the preparation of slides emphasizes that there should be a strict limit to the number of lines of text on a slide. Depending on the guide this is usually between 5 and 7. In addition, a good rule of thumb is that each line should only have 5-7 words. This is very constraining, especially if you are using your slides effectively as notes which you plan to read to your audience. Well, first of all this should not be the purpose of your slides: they are there to help emphasise and illustrate the points that you are making, not as your script. Most of the words in a lecture should be spoken: those that are on the slides are simply signposts or key words to underscore your arguments. Second, if your slides contain virtually all the text you plan to say, they will be impossibly dense and completely dysfunctional as visual aids, being neither visible nor helpful.

The text on your slides should be clear, simple and short. The use of full sentences is rarely required unless you are showing a quotation, and bulleted points are always preferable to prose.

When calculating your number of lines remember to include any header or title line you are using – it's still on the slide and your audience has to look at it and read it – as well as any footer or reference line. Many corporate bodies are compelled for legal reasons to insist that statements are referenced as footnotes on slides, but while they may adhere to the letter of the law they certainly do not comply with its spirit. More often than not these references are unreadable, even by the speaker, as the font size used is so small. It seems obvious to state that there should be no text on your slide that cannot be read, but every day I see slides being used that contain miniscule reference lines at the bottom. If you need references make them readable and keep them as short and simple as possible. Occasionally several references are used – I have counted up to ten on one slide. Again it may be stating the obvious, but don't try to pack too much information into too small a space. If the content of your slide requires ten references to back it up you are probably asking too much of that slide.

Lastly, some lecturers like to use upper rather than lower case lettering. This is presumably done for emphasis, as capitalized words appear to shout from the page or screen. What you need to be aware of, if you do this, is that people read capitalized text significantly more slowly than lower case text. If you want the text on your slides to be as easily read as possible then I suggest you stick to lower case except for normally capitalized letters.

I IS FOR IMAGES

The use of images whether they are photographs, diagrams or graphs, is, in my opinion, the most important use of slides. Words you can say, but pictures you have to show. Your audience will of course be a varied group with different learning styles. Some will get most of their information from listening to what you say, some from reading the text on your slides, while others by looking at the images that you show. Most will use a mixture of sources, but all will have a preference for one or the other. To cater for all these learning styles you have to employ a mixture of media and this includes the use of good images.

GRAPHS

Many of us will use graphs such as histograms, line graphs and scatter plots to illustrate our talks. One golden rule which is often ignored is to define the axes and talk the audience through them. Put simply, graphs are hard to take in and the audience needs time to do so. Look at the example in figure 6.3. Here you should say:

> *This graph shows the relationship between serum cholesterol on the x-axis and death from coronary heart disease on the y-axis. As you can see, as the serum cholesterol increases in the population so does the risk of death — the relationship is not however a straight line but a curve which becomes steeper and steeper as we climb through the cholesterol range.*

Not:

Cholesterol and heart disease are obviously related…

and move on.

Fig. 6.3 Slide showing the relationship between cholesterol and risk of coronary heart disease.

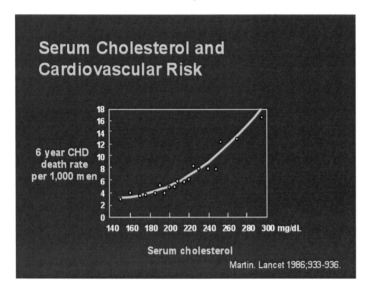

The latter approach took less than 5 seconds and no one in the audience could have looked at the slide and understood its contents, so why bother showing it? If you're giving a talk where the audience is sufficiently sophisticated that they would already be completely familiar with this concept (such as the relationship between cholesterol and heart disease risk) then don't bother showing them a flash graph like this. Slide flashing - showing complex images like graphs so fast that no one can assimilate them - is a particular crime of so-called experts.

All it really says is: "I've got all these slides - I couldn't be bothered sorting through them and preparing an appropriate talk for this specialist audience – well you're not really worth the effort." This also happens a lot with undergraduate teaching where senior academics do not feel the need to adjust their styles to accommodate the needs of their students, preferring to re-use their latest conference presentation on the first year students. Needless to say this is not lecturing, it is simply indolence.

Graphs should, as always, be uncluttered and not contain unnecessary information. It is tempting to scan graphs into your presentations from journal articles or other sources, but inevitably these sources were not designed for projection. As such they will contain additional text or their colour schemes will be difficult to project. It is cumbersome but very worthwhile to redraw the graph so that it suits your presentation and conforms to your style. Occasionally the graph may be so complex that it is impossible to redraw without access to the original data – if this is the case you might ask yourself if you should be showing such a complex image in the first place.

DIAGRAMS

The use of diagrams or figures can greatly enhance a lecture. Often abstract concepts can be represented and made clear by a good diagram. As noted in the case of graphs, the temptation to re-use scanned images without altering them to fit your style should be resisted. If you do have to use a copied image at least take the time to delete or cover up any unnecessary details or associated text. This will make the image much more useful and will allow your audience to concentrate on the relevant part of the image. An example of a raw copied image and a much more audience-friendly one that has been doctored to remove extraneous detail and reconstructed into two simpler slides is shown in figure 6.4.

Fig. 6.4 A complex slide turned into two more audience-friendly versions.

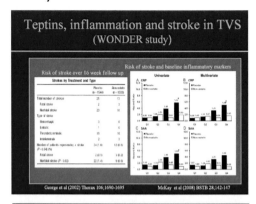

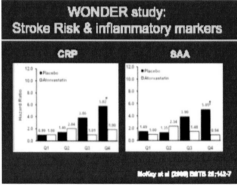

PHOTOGRAPHS

Photographs are essential elements of many lectures. If you are speaking about the History of Art how could you do so without showing slides with photographs of paintings? If you are describing the marketing plan for a new brand of cereal how could you avoid showing photos of the packaging and advertising? Other topics such as financial advice or English literature may not be obvious contenders for the use of photos, but I would strongly urge their use where possible. Slides that only contain text very quickly become tedious – at least they do to me, as I am one of your audience members who learn from a combination of words and pictures. Why not illustrate your talk on Romantic Poetry with a portrait of Shelley, or your lecture on Individual Savings Accounts with a stock photo of a typical family or elderly couple who may be the investors in your case study. Think about how newspapers and magazines do it. Even articles about abstract concepts are wrapped around images that somehow evoke the themes therein. The editors do this to draw your eye to the article. Although your slides should not merely be used for attention grabbing, a carefully selected image may compliment the words you are saying, or the text you are showing, and may make the point more memorable.

P IS FOR PALETTE

As with background designs and text fonts, when it comes to colour schemes, you literally have the full spectrum to choose from. But, some colours and colour combinations work much better than others. For example, it is simply incomprehensible to me why those who make slides continue to insist on using reds. This is not a political statement, merely an acknowledgment of the fact that the colour red – red text, lines or figures – do not project well and are often completely invisible especially if the background chosen is black or blue.

My simple recommendation is that you should avoid the use of red completely. Tried and tested colour schemes are white and/or yellow on dark blue or black backgrounds. You may be particularly prone to purple or green or burnt sienna – of course there is no problem in using alternative background colour schemes, but consider very carefully the corresponding text and graphic colours. Remember around 8% of the men sitting in your audience are colour blind and may have trouble distinguishing your colour schemes especially if they are based on reds and greens. Despite this I cannot count how many times I have seen slides used with red text on a green background. Clearly such a combination should be avoided. Some of these options are illustrated in figure 6.5.

Whatever you choose – a colour scheme that is tried and tested and acceptable to most audiences or something a little more quirky, individual and therefore risky – keep it consistent. Use the same background format and colour scheme throughout your lecture. This will make your presentation more coherent and will allow your audience to relax a little and concentrate on the slide content rather than trying to work out why one slide is blue, the next is yellow with flowers down the side and the third black and white.

E IS FOR EXTRAS

By extras I mean those embellishments that can be added to slides to produce the 'wow' factor. Usually this is in the form of some visual effect, but it may be also be the use of a sound effect or it may be the embedding of a short audio or video file that can be played from within the slide set.

The insertion of audio files into your presentation can be highly innovative and educationally stimulating at one end of the spectrum and deeply irritating at the other. They may even render your lecture faintly ridiculous and memorable for all the wrong reasons. Unless the sound clip is entirely relevant to your lecture, and you are completely confident in its use, don't use it.

Fig. 6.5 Examples of slide colour schemes.

(a) Although red on black might look alright when printed it does not project well and should be avoided

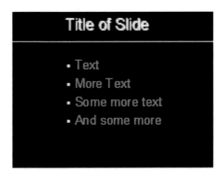

(b) Red on green or vice versa should always be avoided

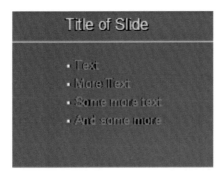

(c) White or yellow on a dark background always works well

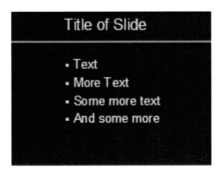

If, for example, you are giving a lecture about President John F. Kennedy and you have a sound clip of one of his key speeches, then its inclusion may give your audience more information than you could ever impart by simply showing a quotation in written words.

However, squeaks, bells, animal sounds, or anything that belongs as a sound effect in a radio play rarely have a place in your lecture. Yes, you may be giving a lecture about the songs of common garden birds, and yes, sound clips of the thrush and the robin would be entirely justified as well as very informative, but you get the point.

One important practical point - if you have sound, either alone or as part of a video make sure you have checked whether the AV system you are using can cope with it. Is the laptop into which you have just inserted your memory stick connected to those speakers in the lecture hall? At the very least try it out beforehand or, if there is one, discuss it with the AV technician. Few experiences are more disconcerting than giving this part of your lecture a big build up, clicking the slide and then being hit by silence - stony, embarrassing, interminable silence. This is especially so if the contents of that audio or video file were critical to the flow of your presentation. It is better if any audio/video is regarded as optional just in case you arrive at the venue and only then discover that you cannot use them.

BUILDS

One major advantage of slides that are generated and shown via a computer, compared with old 35mm slides, is that you have the capacity to animate your slides and in particular to use builds. Building is when you animate the text or images on a slide in such a way that you only reveal part at first and then, as required, you reveal the rest. For example, a bulleted list may not be shown at first in its entirety, but be shown one bullet at a time. The beauty of this approach, from an educational point of view, is that it brings your slides closer to the blackboard style of teaching. We have slowed things down, we are only showing what we are actually talking about rather than a lot of other, for the moment, extraneous text or images, and we can develop arguments step by step. Similarly, if you wish to compare and contrast two graphs or images on the same slide show one and then reveal the other. This allows your audience to direct their attention to each image in turn rather than being confronted with both simultaneously.

For the practicalities of using build techniques and the simple animations I would refer you to the manuals and the online support offered by the suppliers of whichever software package you choose. However, do remember that like everything connected with slides, the use of builds and animation can be overdone. If so, this technique loses its impact and, very quickly, its audience appeal.

SLIDE ADVANCE AND TRANSITIONS

If you are using a slide show to illustrate and enhance your lecture one of the things you must decide on is how the slides will advance and how they will transition.

In most instances you will be in control of your own slides and will have access either to the computer keyboard and mouse, or to a remote control that will allow you to advance and reverse as you need. If, however, you are speaking at a venue that offers neither of these you may have to rely on a third party to control your slides for you. If at all possible try to avoid this as the interminable "Next slide please" becomes very grating on the audience. Also if you have builds or embedded files such as audio or video there will be a roughly 50:50 chance of this working as you had planned it.

When it comes to how the slides transition this will be a decision you make beforehand when you are making up your presentation. The software package you use will allow a variety of transitions from none (the next slide simply appears) to wipes from left, right, top or bottom, and on to a variety of more theatrical effects. You will even have the opportunity to have random effects – a different one for every slide. Please believe me when I say that this is not a good idea. The use of random effects – indeed the use of any exotic effect – diminishes your lecture and dilutes your message. Either use no effect, a fade or a simple wipe, but always in the same direction. As with colour schemes and overall styling, consistency is important. You do not want your slides to overpower and dominate the lecture by dazzling and/or irritating your audience.

WHEN NOTHING IS BEST

Sometimes, even if you intend to use slides, there may be parts of the presentation during which you would like the audience's undivided attention. The best way to do this is to force their eyes on you by turning off the slides. If you are using PowerPoint this is easy. When you are in presentation mode simply hit the 'B' on the keyboard and the screen will go black. Similarly, if you hit the 'W' it will go white. To return to your slides simply hit the key again. Pauses from the slide presentation, like this, can be very useful and allow you to recap important points, perhaps enter into an interactive discussion with the audience, or simply relate an anecdote that requires no visual back-up.

One caveat – if the room lights are dimmed and you blacken the screen it will become very dark and unless you are lit by a podium light the audience is unlikely to be able to see you. The impact may then be somewhat diluted. It is therefore best to use this technique when you also have access to the lighting controls – blacken the screen and raise the lights.

SHOWING MORE THAN ONE SLIDE AT A TIME

Some lecturers adopt the technique of dual or even triple projection. This is when two or in some cases three screens are set up and the audience is confronted with multiple slides at the same time. This was a technique much favoured by American physicians in the 80s and 90s. I have never seen it effectively or proficiently used and, unless the lecturer has a very co-ordinated command of the several slide controllers involved, can descend into a comic *son et lumière*. Of course, it is really just an excuse to show double the amount of information the speaker should be presenting, in an attempt to bludgeon the audience into thinking that the lecturer is smarter than they are.

With the advent or Microsoft PowerPoint and its counterparts this practice has declined, but equally heinous crimes are now committed: the overuse of fonts, colours, and entry and exit effects.

SHARING SLIDES

Once you start making good slides one thing you will have to deal with is the request: "Can I have a copy of your slides?" This is a difficult one. You may have spent many hours preparing your talk, sourcing interesting examples, redrawing graphs and diagrams, identifying appropriate photographs and suddenly you are expected to hand these over – sometimes to a complete stranger. In the past when lecturers used 35mm slides it was much easier to say no, but now you have just walked off the stage and are clutching your memory stick in your hand and your new best friend has his laptop at the ready.

You may take the approach that you simply do not give away your slides as they are your intellectual property. You may have no qualms about it and would happily post them for download to all and sundry from the web. More likely you are somewhere in between – you don't mind sharing some of your slides with some people, especially those who you think might return the favour in your own time of need. My usual response is never to give anyone a memory stick, but to give them my e-mail address and ask them to contact me. If they are serious they will take the time to make contact – although many don't – and then you can send them the slides you are happy to share. You can explain to them that you will send them some of the slides – "not them all" you will emphasise, "because not all the slides are mine to give away". As an excuse this also has the advantage of usually being true.

CASES OF SLIDE CRIME

Anyone who has attended a large conference where there are many and varied speakers or who has, as a student, enjoyed and endured a succession of lecturers, will have witnessed slide crime. Unfortunately it abounds and in some areas it is reaching epidemic proportions. Every witness can describe their own experiences.

These three are real life examples that happened at meetings I attended in just the last year.

1. "This slide is terrible and I apologise, but…." the speaker announces with sham regret and more than a little "well I'm so busy and important I don't really have time to fix it". The slide in question had 46 lines of text – I counted them.

2. "Just look at this part here and ignore the rest." The slide was a photograph of a composite figure from a journal article and had eight separate panels with a different graph in each.

3. "I'm sorry this table is incomplete - I downloaded it from the internet and the last two columns dropped off.

Unfortunately that's the important bit – so I'll just talk you through it." Need I say more?

Ladies and Gentlemen of the jury, the case for the prosecution rests.

OTHER VISUAL AIDS

Although slides are undoubtedly the most widely used visual aids they are not the only ones and this chapter would be incomplete with looking at some others.

OVERHEAD PROJECTION (OHP)

OHP was designed to allow lecturers to project images in a room without the lights turned off. It also allows the lecturer access to a more convenient "blackboard". If this book had been written twenty years ago I would be devoting a whole chapter to the use of overhead projectors and I would be doing so with pleasure because effective use of OHP is one of the best teaching tools around. Indeed, the Nobel Prize winning chemist Harold Kroto and the renowned psychologist Edward de Bono are just two examples of speakers who gave keynote lectures – scintillating, absorbing talks to large conference audiences - entirely using overhead projection.

However, with the rise of PowerPoint and the greater reliance on more complex technology the simple OHP is going out of fashion to such an extent that many lecture rooms now no longer have them. In some cases they have been replaced with overhead video cameras that effectively do the same job, but for a lot more money.

If you are planning on using OHP for your presentation first ensure that the necessary equipment is available and is working. In designing your presentation you will have to follow many of the same rules that apply to the preparation of slides. Each transparency you use should have a consistent and preferably simple format. The text you use, which may be hand-written or generated by a word processor, needs to be clearly readable and of an appropriate size and font. You should ensure that the amount of text used is not a burden to those trying to read it, and that it should be key points and headings rather than a work of prose. Finally you should consider the use of images as these will enhance your presentation and acknowledge and support the different learning styles in your audience.

Lastly, one pitfall to avoid. If you are using an overhead projector and you want to use a pointer, use a pen and point it out on your transparency, not a two metre stick that you use on the screen.

BLACKBOARDS AND WHITEBOARDS

Blackboards have been around longer than any of us. They, their more modern counterparts, the whiteboards, and their even more modern counterparts the interactive whiteboards or screens, effectively serve the same purpose, i.e. to allow the lecturer to produce a live set of visual notes to accompany their lecture. The fact that the blackboard has been updated, rather than discarded, is testament to its usefulness as a teaching aid. Indeed, many would argue that lecturing, and therefore teaching, is best achieved with the combination of an enthusiastic and well-informed human bearing a piece of chalk and a clean blackboard. I have put off discussing it until now because few of you reading this book will ever have used a blackboard and chalk, and probably cannot imagine ever delivering your pearls of wisdom to an audience in this way. The simple reality, however, is that this is the best way to teach. It forces the lecturer to go at a slower pace – if you have to write on a board you will not be able to flash up ten lines of text and move on. Also it forces an economy of style – you will write up key words only and will draw simple diagrams that you feel are really necessary to understand the point being made. Of course it has its deficiencies – you cannot show photographs, and video clips are out of the question, and the state of your clothes after a particularly vibrant session has to be seen to be believed. That said, maybe there is much we can learn here that we can adapt to our other visual aids.

The pace and economy of style can be easily adapted to either OHPs or slides. In the latter, think of your slides as mini blackboards. Imagine each time you show a slide that it is blank and that its contents have to be written or drawn by you while you are talking and only in the duration that you plan to show the slide, which will usually be one minute. This is a very interesting test and one that most slides and their lecturers would fail. But, if you apply this in practice it forces you to keep your slides very simple and spare and therefore much more educationally useful.

FLIP CHARTS

These large paper pads on stands can be very useful, but rarely have a place in the large lecture room as they simply cannot be seen from a distance. Flip charts are much more useful in small group teaching and have an advantage over a simple black or white board in that you can tear off the sheets and hang them around the room to show the development of your argument.

7

WHEN THINGS GO WRONG:

HOW TO AVOID BANANA SKINS

The list of what *can* go wrong when giving a lecture is too long to be funny. However, the list of what is *likely* to go wrong in any given lecture is more manageable and simple steps can be taken to eliminate all but the most unpredictable of calamities.

NERVES

If you forget where you are, if you lose the place, if you drop your notes, if a slide suddenly appears that you had not expected, the silence will be deafening and it will last at least five minutes – or so it will seem. In reality what you perceive as horror will barely register on the audience; what you perceive as five minutes will in reality be around a second or two.

First of all, try to remember this is not a gladiatorial contest; there is no emperor about to pronounce your fate by the turn of his thumb. You are in a room with other people giving a talk. Of course it's important – you wouldn't have spent all that time preparing if it wasn't - but it is just a talk. Pick up your notes and put them back in order, consult them if you've lost your train of thought, or simply say about the errant slide, "Oh what are you doing there?" and move on.

Mistakes – little ones – can be quite comforting to an audience; it shows you're human after all. Big mistakes can be more of a problem and may require a bigger solution. Having a panic attack is difficult to cover up, as is developing an acute illness. It would be easy to advise, "Keep Calm and Carry On" just as the British pre-war poster did, but often that's exactly what you are unable to do (figure 7.1). Channel the panic and start talking to the audience – if you have to leave the lectern or the room, simply explain the situation, make your apologies and leave. If the lecture has gone into freefall because of a technical disaster, again engage the audience. Talk to them about what's happening – "I'm sorry, but there's a lot of smoke coming from the projector so we might want to shut that down for a moment" – think of the audience as the passengers on a jet you are piloting which has been sitting on the tarmac for over an hour and has not yet taken off. Keep them informed and tell the truth – people can be surprisingly forgiving in these circumstances.

Occasionally it will be necessary to abort – nothing else for it but to explain the disaster and apologise. Depending on how far you have got you may be able to salvage the day by having an extended Q&A – or an early tea-break.

For those prone to nerves it is tempting to drink alcohol or take drugs to enhance your performance – don't, because they won't. It may feel as though your powers of persuasion are at their peak and that your wit is more sparkling than ever, but it will be an illusion. Sometimes it may even be obvious to the audience that your Dutch courage has rendered you a little the worse for wear. Neither the lecture nor your reputation will benefit from this – it may even be fatal. "Remember that funny, drunk guy at last year's symposium – whatever happened to him?"

Fig 7.1 British motivational poster which was printed on the eve of World War II in 1939, but which was in fact never used. Its message is a good motto for the lecturer in trouble, but is easier said than done.

WHEN IT'S NOT YOU

Even good drivers get involved in accidents because of other motorists who shouldn't have passed their tests. Similarly, no matter how well you have prepared and no matter how consummate a professional you have become, you can still become the victim of the lecturing equivalent of a rear-ending by being in the wrong place at the wrong time.

Occasionally you will have to share the programme with a terrible speaker. This of course can be no bad thing, for even if you give an average performance you will shine by comparison. However, their antics may directly impact upon you adversely. Often poor speakers have no sense of time and they will run on. If the session is poorly chaired this will eat into your time. On a number of occasions, particularly when I was more junior, I was the victim of this. The chairman would introduce me and, from the podium, would instruct: "In order to get us back on track and not be late for lunch I am sure Dr Gaw will be able to cut his lecture down to 15 minutes." The intended lecture had been 45 minutes and, no, Dr Gaw couldn't; not without a panic attack and a machete. Such on the spot rewriting of a story, which is after all what a lecture is, can be very difficult. If you are faced with this situation you should still give your beginning and your end and leave out most of the filling. Try not to be too truculent about it, although I do personally find this difficult as I hate waste. All the time and effort that went into crafting the presentation are not only wasted, but so is the opportunity to give a good, rather than a mediocre, lecture.

Your co-speakers may also have committed a range of other misdemeanours. They may not have dimmed the lights which were in their control, used the microphones or the slide advance or the laser pointer properly, stood in the right place or even knew what they were talking about. You have to rise above all this and give the lecture you had prepared in the way you had planned. Do not be embarrassed about rearranging things when you get up to speak: "I think for my slides I'll need to dim the lights a little." If the previous presentation has been an unmitigated disaster, perhaps you might begin: "I must thank the last speaker for an engaging discussion – now I would like to give you my, rather different, take on the topic." Or even, "If you don't mind I'll try and spend the next twenty minutes repairing the intellectual damage wrought by the previous imbecile." Don't, however, say that, even if you're thinking it.

Worst of all, however, is when you are on a programme and one of the previous speakers – most notably the one immediately before you – effectively gives your lecture for you. This can and does happen and it is usually the fault of the organizers who have poorly briefed the different speakers, or may be accounted for by the simple arrogance of some speakers who pay no attention to anyone or anything else in the programme. When this happens it can be very difficult. You are expected to rise and give a lecture which may be very similar in content, argument and conclusions to the one before. You have really only two options: you either completely ignore what has just happened and carry on regardless or you acknowledge what you will euphemistically term the "overlap", but will suggest that these points are so important that they merit repeating and looking at in a slightly different way. I have done both and neither feels particularly comfortable, but you do not have the time or opportunity to make up a new lecture.

One way of avoiding this is to ask for the full programme beforehand and not just the title and brief for your own talk. Look for potential overlaps and suggest these to the organizers. If possible talk to the speakers who will present before you and ask to see their slides, at the same time offering them sight of yours.

Be as helpful as you can if one of the other speakers asks about the contents of your presentation – they are only doing what you should be doing too. Remember, occasionally you might be the culprit and find yourself covering the topics that the following speaker thought were hers. Simple co-operation can help avoid this.

LACK OF AN AUDIENCE

If you are waiting patiently to speak and there is a conspicuous lack of an audience, ask yourself some simple questions. Am I in the right place? Is this the right day or time? Am I really this bad? Assuming that word has not got around that your lectures are the academic equivalent of paint drying you must assume that something is amiss. If you have a captive audience like a university class, none of whom have shown up then safely assume you are in the wrong. If, however, the prospective audience will comprise of people taking some time out of their busy schedules to come and listen to you voluntarily, it may just be your unlucky day.

The only thing worse than no one turning up, of course, is when one person turns up. If there are two you can just about call it an audience, but a single soul is a problem. He or she will be even more embarrassed than you, so you have to decide between yourselves whether the show goes on or whether you simply retire for a (short) chat to the bar. And yes, it has happened to me and yes I did give the lecture, but I did do it sitting down with my jacket off in a vain attempt to lighten the formality of it all. My audience, or I should say she, did seem to appreciate that I had bothered. Similarly, I was surprised that she chose to stay, but all turned out well and she thanked me for sharing some new information with her in such a personalised way.

DISRUPTION

If there is disruption to a lecture because of someone talking loudly that isn't me, I initially try to ignore it, as often the audience will deal with it on my behalf. A loud "Ssh!" from an adjacent member of the audience may be enough to suppress the insurrection. If it persists you may have to take action. As a lecturer, remember, you have considerable power, and simply pausing and fixing the offender with a stare can be enough. The pause itself and your silence will make their chatter even more audible and hopefully embarrassing. Finally, if that has not worked, you may need to say something: "Well, either I can give the lecture or you can, but I don't think we should both try. Shall I stop or shall you?" Ideally it should not have reached this stage, but if it does you must always stay in control.

Chatting is only one form of disruption. The mobile phone can be another source of irritation to both the speaker and the audience. Mobile phones that go off, usually with some ridiculous ring tone, during a lecture can be surprisingly off-putting. To avoid this, either you or the chair should ask the audience to ensure that their mobiles are turned off or put on to silent mode for the duration of the lecture, "as a courtesy to the speaker and to the others in the audience." If this happens make sure you switch your own phone off too: can't have the pot calling the kettle black! The ultimate mobile misdemeanour, however, is when one of the audience receives a call and chooses to take it. There is little to do here other than pause and hope that their surrounding audience members rip them limb from limb on your behalf.

Until now I have only considered auditory disruptions, but in extreme situations things can get physical. As lecture attendance in most institutions and certainly at meetings and conferences is not compulsory, it may be expected that everyone who is in the room has chosen to be there. As such you should not expect the level of disruption and inattention you might encounter in some secondary education settings.

However, undergraduates can be boisterous and at times silly. Occasionally things will be thrown. While I could probably cope with a paper aeroplane and perhaps even incorporate the symbolism into my talk I choose to adopt a zero tolerance approach to this: when something – anything – is thrown at me, I stop, collect my things and leave. I suggest you do the same.

THE UNEXPECTED

We have covered the main problems you are likely to encounter when giving a lecture, but what of that long list of things that *can* happen. All speakers have to be prepared for the unexpected. As far as anecdotes go I have to restrain myself here as I have enjoyed many unanticipated interruptions or distractions to my talks over the years. However, here are three of the best:

At a meeting in Los Angeles, one of my audience suddenly got up half way through my talk, came to the front of the lecture room, lay on the floor and starting doing yoga. On another occasion, in Indonesia, not only did my chairman's mobile phone ring during my lecture but he proceeded to take the call – all while still being attached to his microphone. And, finally, I once lost half my audience during a lecture I was giving in Vietnam because of an earthquake –a small one. For the half who remained behind I kept going – spirit of the blitz and all that.

While these examples are funny, they won't happen to you – different ones will. How do you prepare for them? Well, you can't – all you can do is prepare your talk as well as you can and above all maintain a sense of humour, because let's face it most things are really quite funny when you start to think about them seriously.

SOURCES OF OFFENCE

It should really go without saying that the content and style of your lectures should not be offensive – at least not intentionally. Sometimes we will be inadvertently rude or disrespectful of either our hosts or our audiences, as a result of our ignorance of local culture. That is bad enough but to do so knowingly, either in an attempt to be provocative or to demonstrate an independence of mind is, in my opinion, crass.

RACISM

Racism is a crime and most institutions and companies in which you may find employment will have corporate policies in place for dealing with complaints of this nature. Think about what you are saying and the images you are showing in your lectures and you will never have to find out what the unpleasant side of the table at a disciplinary hearing feels like.

SEXISM

If it was not for some of the antics I have witnessed in lectures delivered by men, I would find it ridiculous and more than a little patronising to suggest that your lectures should not be sexist. A simple acknowledgement that more than half of the world's population is female should be enough to ensure that lectures delivered in the 21st century are free of sexism. This is not political correctness; it is simple human decency. Occasionally, though less often, sexism works in the other direction – female lecturers showing disrespect and disregard for men. This is often seen as amusing, but it is equally wrong and just as offensive.

There have been distinguished female writers, musicians, scientists and doctors as well as ones who were men. There have also been infamous female murderers, despots and villains as well as those who were men. It would be a mistake to ignore any of them just because they were women.

Quite apart from your content, your style may also be sexist. You should avoid, if possible, the use of gender specific pronouns, and perhaps consider why the example you are using is a *he* rather than a *she*.

AGEISM

Age is another area where it is possible to be inconsiderate and casually offensive. Whether it be the young or the old do think about how you are referring to them, or indeed speaking to them if they are in the audience. In general, do not generalise. All young adults are not feckless layabouts, just as all older adults are not bewildered incontinents. Some of them are, but not all of them, and probably not the ones attending your talk.

Cultural and religious sensitivity

As outlined in Chapter 8, when we are speaking to foreign audiences we have to take note of certain cultural taboos and be mindful of our behaviour and our etiquette. Even in your home country you may be speaking to mixed groups of people, some of whom are from racial, ethnic or religious minorities. In the UK we live and work in a multi-cultural society and most of us should be able to access a range of personal experiences to help us deal with this aspect of giving lectures. As in all the examples outlined above, sensitivity is the key.

8

TALKING AROUND THE WORLD:

LECTURES WITH AIR MILES

One of the wonderful things about lecturing is that it can take you around the world. If your reputation grows you may expect to be invited to speak at meetings and conferences in places you would not normally have the opportunity to visit. When I started working with a new research group I asked what I should do first and one of my new colleagues quipped, "Get a passport." I have thoroughly enjoyed my travels and have met some fascinating and colourful people. Some have even become lifelong friends.

Of course, to enjoy lecturing in foreign parts you have to understand the challenges that such speaking bring. In this chapter I want to consider several important areas, which will allow you to prepare appropriately for your lecture abroad and to savour the experience.

FOREIGN AUDIENCES

Some audiences will be multi-national, as at a major international symposium. Others will be from a single country and it can sometimes be useful to be aware of certain national characteristics. Some national and cultural stereotypes are heartless and fictitious; others are useful and surprisingly accurate. The following have been forged from my own experience.

Rarely does anything start on, or run to, time in a country where they habitually drink wine at lunchtime. This may not necessarily be a cause and effect relationship, but I suspect there is a strong association.

Australians are a tough audience – in my experience the toughest of all – with no mercy for anyone they feel may be bull-shitting them, but if you pass muster they are excellent hosts, and of course any opportunity to visit this amazing continent of a country must never be missed.

Far Eastern audiences are generally very gracious and completely silent when it comes to question time. However, they are not disinterested, merely anxious not to embarrass you. As an invited speaker you are an honoured guest and as such must be accorded every courtesy, and that does not include being asked difficult questions or being challenged in any way.

Americans are so diverse as to be impossible to generalize, but they are often suspicious of anything that's not American. If you are not a native, or your work was not carried out in the States, be prepared for scepticism. Being British can be an advantage however, as they like the accent. Being Scottish, if you can pull it off, is even better – although some of us have an advantage there in actually being Scottish. American chairs do like to give very full introductions and if you give them your full CV they will read it out including the details of the High School you attended and even your children's names. One other point about American meetings that often throws British speakers – when it says the lecture starts at 10.00am it means just that, not a couple of minutes, or even a couple of hours, later. This is in contrast to the places where they drink wine at lunchtime, but that's where we came in.

FOREIGN VENUES

LP Hartley famously said the past was a foreign country; they do things differently there. Perhaps he had tried to give lectures in a few foreign venues for they certainly will be doing things very differently when you arrive to give your lecture. Do not expect the same equipment you are used to at home. It might be better or worse, but it is unlikely to be the same. The rules of social discourse will be unfamiliar as will be the etiquette for attendance at your lecture. You may find timings elastic rather than fixed, and you will be surprised by just how many people smoke.

Foreign venues may be in University Departments, Conference Centres or Hotels, just as they may be at home, but because of their unfamiliarity you should take a little longer to accustom yourself to your surroundings, and the equipment, than you would normally. Try not to view the differences as obstacles, but rather they should prompt you to savour the moment. And, while we are on the subject of savouring, a word of wisdom about what you might be offered to eat and drink.

Before your lecture, don't eat seafood, have ice-cubes in your drinks or have salad that might have been washed in the local river. It is just about impossible to give a convincing lecture while acutely aware of your gastrointestinal transit time. If you have travelled all the way to Venezuela, or Egypt or Sri Lanka to give a talk, it seems a pity to miss it because of an errant prawn, or because you brushed your teeth with the tap water. After the lecture knock yourself out - you'll only have a long-haul flight home to contend with and having vomiting and diarrhoea on one of those is never a problem, is it?

FOREIGN ETIQUETTE

To be a professional providing any service in another country is a privilege. When that service is education it is doubly so; for you are likely to learn as much as your audience. As an invited speaker you will be a guest and will enjoy many kindnesses from your hosts. Being a guest, however also brings with it considerable responsibility. Quite apart from being professionally worth the bother – i.e. being a good lecturer – you should also behave yourself and you should never intentionally embarrass your hosts. One way to prevent this is to avoid discussing topics that may be politically or religiously sensitive, especially if, as is often the case, you don't really know what you're talking about. Unintentional embarrassment is more difficult to avoid, but can be minimized by learning a bit about the culture you are about to sample. You will usually be forgiven for being a foreign oaf in most countries, but there is no point in being mindlessly offensive, and any attempt you can make to conform to the local niceties is always appreciated. Here are just some examples.

The etiquette associated with the exchange of business cards can be byzantine and varies from region to region. First of all make sure if you are travelling abroad that you have some.

They should be good quality and preferably carried in a small card case. In Asia, particularly Japan, the exchange of business cards is almost ritualistic. They should be offered and received with both hands, they should be studied and fondled and they should never be slipped into your pocket, written on or even discarded as this will show profound disrespect. Any cards you receive should be put with due reverence into your card case.

When dining in many cultures, if you are the guest, you will be expected to start eating first. Bear this in mind if you feel things are going rather slowly. Your hosts are simply being polite and waiting on you. In the Middle East do not attack a finger buffet with your left hand – they reserve that for quite another function. Similarly, don't ask for the wine list – even if they do drink privately it will inevitably be a source of awkwardness.

Bodily functions such as sneezing, coughing, and belching are also fraught with difficulty. Nose blowing in public is particularly disgusting to the Japanese (I have to say I'm not too keen on it either), while belching in some Middle Eastern societies is positively to be encouraged.

Some cultural taboos are even more difficult to predict. For example, sitting or resting your bottom on a table or desk will be considered deeply offensive by the Maori in New Zealand. While in Iran a simple thumbs-up sign will be regarded as an offensive insult.

There are many websites and books which can provide specific information regarding the etiquette of working in different countries and several useful ones are listed in the appendices at the end of this book.

Remember however, that as long as you take with you the simple manners that you were taught as a child; as long as you behave yourself and avoid getting drunk; as long as you act with an air of respect, you will be forgiven almost any *faux pas* and may even be invited back.

A FEW WORDS IN THE LOCAL TONGUE

The device of starting a lecture to a foreign audience by saying a few words in their local language is well tried and tested, but just because it is common does not mean that it will not succeed time and again. One word of warning: if you do not know the language at all, get advice from a reliable source – everyone will welcome a native English speaker trying, no matter how badly, to speak the local language. I have found myself saying "Good Morning" in the evening, "Goodbye" when I was trying to say hello and casting aspersions on the parenthood of the chairman with all the innocence of a faun. But, say it in Russian, Greek, Japanese or Portuguese and you'll get a round of applause before you've said a word of your talk. This, the ultimate ice-breaker, demonstrates that you have tried and audiences, even hard ones, find that irresistible.

TRANSLATION

Translation is obviously most commonly used in parts of the world where English is not well-understood. In my experience this has been mainly Hispanic areas both in Europe and Latin America as well as some areas of Asia, especially China. Of course you may also find yourself attending an international conference in the UK or the US, where for the benefit of a large section of the audience there may be translation services. Simultaneous translation is an expensive option for conference organizers and it is therefore most commonly used at industry sponsored events and where the size of the audience merits it.

SIMULTANEOUS TRANSLATION

Picture the United Nations – some diplomat is addressing the Security Council and a bank of translators is ensconced behind glass, wired up and racked with concentration attempting to get every nuance of the language they are hearing from the floor into the language they are speaking. The audience, earpieces in place, is watching the speaker, seeing her lips move, but hearing the measured tones of a linguist. Well, it's not exactly like that in our world, but it's close.

If your lecture is going to be simultaneously translated there are a number of important considerations. Overall, you should construct and deliver your talk with the translation process in mind, not as an inconvenience to you and therefore an afterthought. There are a number of important things to consider:

1. Think carefully about the length of your talk

You will have to speak more slowly than normal as both a courtesy to the translators and more importantly because a number of languages require significantly more words to say the same things as in English. For example, in Spanish your translator will have to say 20-30% more words and syllables than you are saying in English for you both to be saying the same thing. Because of this you will have to pace your lecture differently – instead of say 30 slides for a 30 minute talk I would suggest only 25.

2. Talk to the translators before the lecture

A heart sink moment occurred once at a meeting in Latin America where my lecture was to be simultaneously translated into Spanish and Portuguese. I took the time beforehand to seek out the Spanish translator, who turned out to be a bilingual physician grateful to have some time to go through the presentation and iron out any potential wrinkles in the translation. I then sought the Portuguese translator, only to be told, "Oh, she doesn't speak English". Now, I'm no expert in linguistics but it seemed to me to be unnecessarily challenging to embark on the simultaneous translation of a lecture from English into Portuguese while only having the command of one of the languages. My face was clearly a picture of puzzlement and concern, for my Spanish translator quickly explained, "I will translate you into Spanish and she will listen to me and translate my translation into Portuguese." This did not provide me with the reassurance that was intended. I was confident that the Spanish translation would be competent, but goodness only knows what the Brazilians in the audience were hearing.

Nonetheless, this does underscore the need to speak to translators if at all possible beforehand. Remember your talk will only be as good as their translation, for effectively they are the ones giving your talk. The slides will be yours, as will the gestures, but the voice will be theirs.

Your chat to the translators may help them check on a few key things in your presentation, it may help them gauge your accent and it may be simply reassuring for all concerned.

3. Have a print-out of your slides

If possible, give the translators a print out of your slides. Translators are often so badly positioned or so focused on the audio that they either cannot or will not see your slides. A print out may again help the translation along.

4. Remember you need an earpiece too

The translator will usually back-translate for you into English the Chair's introduction and any questions from the floor. Don't wear the earpiece during your talk – it may distract you unnecessarily and may also interfere with the microphone and anyway it's just too many wires all at once.

5. Jokes don't work well unless they're visual

I am sure it is possible to translate funny stories from one language into another, but it certainly cannot be done simultaneously. Puns are especially untranslatable and many jokes depend on understanding a common culture or social stereotypes that may be unknown to your audience or your translator. If you like to include funnies in your lecture, either to make a point or to lighten the subject, make sure that they are sufficiently international or indeed non-national to work. Look for what's common to all and if possible rely on the visual, and remember no matter what you are talking about everybody thinks penguins are funny.

6. Dispense with any abbreviations or acronyms

These will often be mistranslated with anything from amusing to catastrophic results. If your field relies on abbreviations, like many science subjects, spend some time giving the term in full the first time you use it.

7. Avoid colloquialisms and idioms

This may be obvious, but sometimes we use colloquialisms without even knowing it. Also our speech is normally peppered with idiomatic language that undoubtedly enriches it, but can also make it incomprehensible to those whose first language is not English. Transliteration of the term 'Out of sight, out of mind' into Russian and back again into English by a computer famously came out as 'Invisible maniac'. Try and stick to very plain English and make especially sure the text on your slides is equally unadorned.

8. Don't assume the translators understand what you are going to talk about

One Japanese translator asked me just before my lecture, "A stroke – that's a heart attack isn't it?" It's easy in such a setting to say "Stuff it – that's their problem." But, of course, it isn't – it's yours – they are, after all, your voice and your lecture will be judged by how clear and meaningful their words are, not yours.

SEQUENTIAL TRANSLATION

This has only happened in my personal experience in the Far East and consists of each of your sentences being translated one by one as you say them. In practice there will usually be someone else on the stage with you - apparently the other half of your lecturing double act. You will say a line and then he or she will say it again in the appropriate language. To say this is cumbersome is an understatement. There is no possibility of spontaneity and all style will be drained out of your lecture. The presentation will also, of course, take twice as long. Again take this into account and make your lecture concise and if possible more visual than usual. At least your slides will be your own. This approach is often used in academic settings as it is much less expensive for organizers, requiring no special equipment, other than the services of a willing bilingual colleague. However, it does not work well. It is a great challenge to keep any rhythm going to your lecture, losing momentum after every sentence as you stand waiting for the translation to be made.

A PERSONAL ASIDE

This might not really be the place for it, but please accept some words of personal advice regarding business travel. If you do get the opportunity to visit wonderful foreign cities and exotic locations, always take the opportunity to see something other than the airport, the hotel and the lecture room. I have colleagues who have been to Paris and never set foot outside the conference hotel; others who have been to Manhattan and couldn't tell you the difference between an Avenue and a Street. Some have been to Sydney and have yet to see the Opera House and others who have been to Rio and never danced the samba. Years later you will never remember the lecture you gave, but you will still be able to tell your grandchildren about the first time you saw the Pyramids, what it felt like to stand on the Acropolis, what the view was like across Hong Kong from the Peak at night or what it smelt like in the Grand Bazaar of Istanbul. Don't let anyone tell you it's all about work.

9

GETTING PAID:

BEING A PRO

Lectures comes in a variety of shapes and sizes. How you construct your lectures as well as how you deliver them will vary from person to person and setting to setting. Similarly the rewards for lecturing will vary greatly and the only rule that applies is that there is absolutely no correlation between the amount of effort put in and the rewards that come out – at least in financial terms.

Some will lecture as part of their jobs – university and college staff, of course, fall into this category – and their salaries are at least in part paid to recompense their efforts in teaching. Unfortunately, many university lecturers in my experience view their lecturing duties as nothing more than an inconvenience that distracts them from their real job, and the one they believe they are paid to do – research. Nevertheless, if lecturing is part of your job description you are being paid to do it.

For others lecturing will be an aside to their main professional role rather than a daily occurrence. Here it is not as obvious that the lecturing is part of your paid employment, but it is certainly part of your wider professional remit.

Then, there are those who are invited to speak, usually because of their professional status and knowledge, but nevertheless completely separate from their day job. Into this category falls a wide range of speaking opportunities. These range from addressing charitable bodies to providing consultancies for industry, with various forms of freelance work in between.

In the consultancy category the opportunity to earn money from your lecturing becomes a reality and with it a whole new range of considerations. Questions such as: "How much should I charge?", "What will they pay?", "How much am I worth?" come to the fore and only some of them are relevant.

First let's get the notion of worth out of your mind. It is a basic rule of market economies that a service is only worth what a client is willing to pay and has no true and absolute value. If this were not true would premier league footballers get paid 200 times more than NHS nurses? With lecturing it's no different. You will never get paid what you are 'worth', only what you can negotiate. But, where do you start? Often in such circumstances the stock advice is to ask around and seek the counsel of your colleagues. If you do try this you will probably quickly hit a series of brick walls. People do not like talking about money and they like talking about their earnings from consultancy even less.

WHAT TO CHARGE

You have to be able to answer the question from a client: "How much is your honorarium?", and to develop an appropriate fee scale for your services. Some sort of sliding scale is needed, for you cannot realistically expect to get the same for a half hour talk in your local institution as for spending 3 days travelling to, and speaking at, an international industry sponsored symposium, even if the same company is sponsoring both events. You have to take account of your time, whether you will need to take time off work, what amount of research and preparation will be required to construct the lecture and whether there are any additional commitments associated with the lecture, such as running a workshop afterwards or preparing and editing a publishable transcript of your lecture.

Often, you will be invited to speak and the honorarium will be set by the organizer beforehand and will be presented as a *fait accompli*. This is fine if the figure is in your ballpark. It's even better if it is more than you usually charge in which case you should smile graciously and accept. But, if it's below your minimum what do you do?

Like many negotiations the answer to this depends on your bargaining position. If the organizers want *you*, rather than someone else *like you*, then you can reasonably ask for the figure to be revised upwards. But, if you can be replaced by a cheaper option you will be and swiftly – also you may acquire a reputation as expensive. This is no bad thing if you have sufficient cachet to merit it, but try to gauge the market and, put bluntly, try not to push your luck. Former US President Bill Clinton is reputed to earn over US$ 200,000 for each lecture. Former British Prime Minister, Tony Blair, apparently shared his thoughts from the podium with the Chinese for £200,000. Apparently the going rate if you are a Nobel Laureate is US$ 25-50,000 a pop. At a recent hospital lunchtime meeting I got two tuna sandwiches and a book token for £10. So it does vary depending on who you are, what you are and who the client is.

Depending on your background there may be standard hourly rates for consultancy work set out by your professional body. For example, in medicine the British Medical Association has a simple guide to hourly rates for a variety of activities, and clients will often quote these to you to defend the fees they offer. Sometimes, this approach is mean-spirited as it fails to acknowledge the simple fact that a one hour lecture does not take one hour of your time. The preparation time must be factored in. Travelling time is a little more problematic and I certainly know some lecturers who charge for every minute they are out of the office. I think this approach is hard to justify as travelling time is often down time where you may either be able to relax or work on other things not related directly to the lecture.

Like all market situations, if you are to sell your services successfully as a lecturer, your price has to be one that the market can bear. Ideally you should be viewed as good value for money by prospective clients, but this is a subjective assessment based not only on what you charge, but also the quality of the product. First and foremost you should strive to be good, then good to work with and only then good value for money. The latter will inevitably follow from the former.

It is relatively exhausting having to negotiate for every lecture. If at all possible it is easier, and much more efficient, to negotiate with a client for a series of lectures. In this way a price can be set for each lecture and that price gets paid without redress to further negotiation each time. Alternatively, some clients may choose to contract you as a consultant and pay for a series of lectures up front, e.g. 6 over the course of a year. Again the negotiation of such a package deal saves everyone time and is to be preferred to re-arguing your case on every occasion.

I know lecturers who have acted as consultants and earned considerable sums on which they have neglected to pay tax. I also know some colleagues who have been the subjects of Inland Revenue audits. And, yes they are one and the same. Companies who pay for lecturing services as well as sending you a nice cheque also inform the Inland Revenue that they have paid you. Thus, consultancy work is not invisible and must be fully declared on your tax returns – to do otherwise is both foolish and illegal.

CONTRACTS

When agreeing to speak for a fee you will routinely be asked to sign a contract. Unless you are a lawyer (and probably even if you are) these documents are turgid and uninviting. In fact most of you thought about skipping over this section, admit it. Most of us simply cut to the chase and find the dotted line on which to sign. Mistake. At the very least check that the fee is as arranged and that other details are as you expect.

Perhaps after you have negotiated to speak for one hour at an event the organizers now expect you to be interviewed on film or to chair a workshop session in addition while you're there. Add-ons like these happen regularly and while they often pose no real problem there should be additional fees for such activities. Similarly, these add-ons may happen at the event itself without ever being mentioned in the contract. If so, the fact that you have read the contract will be your protection and a useful way out of what can become an awkward situation. "I'm sorry, but there was no mention of this additional workshop in the contract you sent me – will I need to sign something else before I agree to it?" It can be difficult and embarrassing to start haggling with a local representative of the organization who has engaged you, especially when they have been poorly briefed. Reverting back to the contract makes you sound professional and business like, but you can only do so if you have taken a little time to read it in the first place.

CANCELLATION FEES

You may be invited to give a talk, the date is set, the preparatory work done, the lecture created and then out of the blue the whole thing is cancelled. Where do you stand? Again the contract may be helpful here. If there are no cancellation policies detailed there should be, and you may wish to suggest them. I work on the basis that if the cancellation happens after I have done the work and possibly turned down other offers in order to deliver the lecture in question, I charge the full fee. In practice this would be within three days of the event. Before that, I try to be flexible and vary my response depending on the circumstances. If the meeting is merely being postponed then no charge will ensue; if however I have already booked travel I will charge for that.

If the cancellation is entirely outside the organizers' control again I think you have to be reasonable. Recently I was prevented from flying to a meeting because of bad weather. Although I had spent time preparing the lecture and could have charged for my time I chose not to. That gesture of goodwill paid off, for rather than simply rescheduling the lecture at a later, more clement, season the organizers invited me to give a three lecture tour instead.

TRAVEL EXPENSES

In addition to a fee, it is essential that you are able to recover travel and subsistence costs as these may be considerable especially if you are attending an international meeting. Again the contract should detail what you will be entitled to claim.

It is no use moaning after the event that your expenses for that night in the hotel bar have been turned down when the contract clearly stated that only your room and breakfast would be chargeable.

Again you must read the contract and never assume that any two organizations will follow the same rules. If the contracted expenses do not meet your anticipated needs ask for them to be changed. If they want you, there may be room for manoeuvre – if not, there won't be.

SIMPLE PRACTICALITIES

If you have agreed to speak at a meeting it is important that as a professional you ensure that you can deliver what is asked of you. If you have to book your own travel or get yourself to the venue make sure you do so in plenty of time. Also make sure you have the full details of the venue including its postcode (for sat-nav purposes) and telephone number. Also make sure you have a contact telephone number for the organizer and that they have yours.

It may be left to you to do the asking about the venue facilities – e.g. whether there is a computer, screen, projector, whiteboard, OHP or whatever you need. Those who invited you, the organizers of the meeting, can be surprisingly uninterested in such details, but then it's not them who have to stand up and give the lecture, it's you. If you cannot visit the venue beforehand to check it out you may have to check its website or phone its conference manager. Remember if you turn up and cannot give your lecture because you assumed that someone would organize a projector, it's not their fault, it's yours. You will look unprofessional as you start blaming everyone but yourself, and more importantly you are unlikely to be used as a speaker again.

As for your slides – you may be required to provide these in advance as discussed in Chapter 1, or you may have to bring them on a memory stick or a laptop. If you need to bring your laptop remember to pack an appropriate international adaptor, if you are travelling abroad as these can be very difficult to find when you arrive. If flying abroad to give your lecture never ever put your laptop, your memory stick or indeed anything to do with your lecture in your checked luggage for you will never see it again. In these circumstances the baggage handlers at London Heathrow or Paris Charles de Gaulle or Chicago O'Hare will have more chance of giving your lecture than you.

FINAL THOUGHTS

In the Introduction to this book I defined different kinds of lecturers. When it comes to consultancy work the most valued by far are the "Spencer Tracy's". Yes, you will see a lot of tarts and seagulls on your travels, but that is only because there are not enough Spencer Tracy's to go round. Be the mature, consummate professional who is well-prepared and does a good job without fuss or drama and you will be in high demand. Organizers of meetings hate working with tarts and seagulls, but they are forced to out of necessity. Offer them an alternative – a low maintenance pro – and you will be as busy as you want to be.

10

TOP TIPS FOR A GREAT TALK:

LECTURING WITH 'E'S

How should you give a lecture? With ease, or at least with 'E's. There are seven key things you should remember and they all conveniently start with the letter 'E'.

EXPERTISE

It should almost go without saying that to give an effective lecture on any topic you must first have command of that topic. Whether you are expounding on differential calculus, Latin poetry or the clinical management of cholesterol disorders, you must first know what you are talking about and have something worth saying on the subject. It is unlikely that you would have been invited to give a lecture on a topic on which you are not familiar, but occasionally things go awry. Perhaps through misunderstanding or in some cases departmental desperation you may find yourself in charge of a lectern in front of an unfamiliar group with someone else's slides and a very dry throat. If you are forced into such a situation you can only try your best, but your audience probably deserved better and that alone should be your stimulus to ensure it doesn't happen again.

In most other settings you will know your subject, but again, because your audience deserves your best, you should ensure that your knowledge is up to scratch. You do not have to be the acknowledged world expert on the subject, but you do have to know more than the audience and you have to have prepared. This may involve simply brushing up on a few facts that have lain in a dusty corner of your mind since you learned them yourself, or it may involve a lot of background research and reading to ensure you are absolutely up to date. It will depend on the lecture, the topic and, of course, the audience.

ENTHUSIASM

If you are not enthusiastic about your subject and about your lecture how can you expect anyone in the audience to be? We have all been to those dull, boring lectures where the speaker drones on and really looks as if he or she would rather be somewhere else. Well, that's not how you want to be remembered. Put a spring in your step and a smile on your face, and let the audience see that you think what you are talking about is not just interesting, but fascinating. Any topic, even if it is superficially dry, can be brought to life by an enthusiastic approach. Part of your job is to identify those elements in your subject that fuel your own enthusiasm and transmit that to your audience.

A significant part of enthusiasm is related to the energy you can generate in the room. Lecturers are people and, as with anyone else you meet, they are either transmitters or drains – you are either warmed by their almost solar radiance, or you are chilled as they extract every last ounce of energy from you. Make sure you are filled to overflowing with positive energy when you speak and it will spill over into the audience. Everything you then say or do will have an added glow. Yes, I know it sounds as if I have slipped into an airport book-stall self-help paperback, but it's simply true. If you stand there and look as if you don't want to be there; if you speak as if you couldn't really care less; if you answer questions as if you resent them, then you will soak the energy from the room. If, instead you lift your voice, vary and modulate your pitch and tone when speaking, move around, use your hands, and really just look as if you are pleased to be there, then your audience will respond to your transmission of energy and will become more energetic in return. You will definitely feel more tired at the end of such a performance – you are using up more of your own energy – but you will have given a much better lecture.

EXPLANATIONS

The contents of your lecture cannot simply be factual. Of course you do have to impart facts, but these can also be found, perhaps more easily, in textbooks or on the internet. Your job is more complex and subtle than dispensing factual knowledge – you also have to explain. This will involve mixing your factual discourse with pauses and asides to clarify and if necessary to elaborate. The form of your explanations will vary with your subject, but will often consist of rephrasing technical terms and expressions in a different form of language. "In other words..." you may begin, thus signposting to your audience that an explanation is now coming. "Let's look at that from another angle..." or "Now, let's think about what that actually means..." are other segues into an explanation. In all of these examples we will be using different language – perhaps just a simpler vocabulary – to help explain the concept.

EXAMPLES

Many of the things you will be teaching in your lecture will be new and abstract. They may not be obvious to anyone coming to the subject for the first time, and they may not seem immediately relevant. In order to bring the theoretical and the abstract back to reality, use concrete examples to illustrate your points. In medicine this might be the use of clinical case studies where you describe a particular patient; in English it may be the reading of passages from specific authors to illustrate the use of metaphor; in Music it may be the playing of excerpts from Joplin to help your audience understand the meaning of syncopation. The examples will vary from subject to subject but the principle remains, that by illustrating an often abstract concept with concrete examples you will help your audience to understand that concept better.

EMPHASIS

In any educational encounter there are key points that have to be conveyed and understood. For your audience to know what these are you have to use emphasis. You are an expert and know what is most important in your subject, but your audience may not. In your 45 minute lecture you may cover a lot of ground and unless you clearly identify what the key messages are they may be lost in the mist of examples, anecdotes and witticisms sprinkled throughout your talk.

Your most important tool for emphasis is your voice. Varying the tone and pace of your delivery – usually deepening and slowing it, perhaps even pausing – will serve to stress particular points. This technique will be backed-up by appropriate visual aids that clearly identify the key points. Most obviously this will be done by a summary slide listing the main take-home messages from the lecture. It might also been done, throughout the talk, with signpost slides that highlight that a key point has just been made. Any handout you provide should serve to emphasise further these key points.

When preparing your lecture be conscious of the key points you want to get across – indeed they should be the first things you write down on your plan. Depending on the length of your lecture you will be able to deal with different amounts of information and deliver a different number of key points. But, whatever the length of your talk you will be able to cover less ground than you might think. In a 10 minute talk have 1-2 key points, in a 30 minute talk 3-4 and in a 50 minute lecture around 5. You will be tempted to put in more, but your lecture will be clearer, less cluttered and much more effective if you follow this guide.

ENTERTAINMENT

The Canadian Communication Theorist and Academic, Marshall McLuhan, said: "Anyone who tries to make a distinction between education and entertainment doesn't know the first thing about either." I think there probably is a distinction, but perhaps not one that makes a difference. What is certainly true is that education without an element of entertainment is a dry exercise. I am not suggesting you have to don a clown suit, hire a unicycle or hone a stand-up comedy routine, but I am suggesting that you think up ways to make your lectures enjoyable in more ways than simple intellectual stimulation. Humour is the most obvious form of entertainment you can use. Making your audience laugh at your jokes or at pictures, cartoons or videos is one sure way of raising the temperature in the room and bringing your lecture to life. But, it does not have to be laughter. Engaging stories and anecdotes can tease an audience to the edges of their seats. Carefully chosen visuals can delight, soften or rouse an audience as required. As you can see entertainment is undoubtedly about manipulation. The entertainer can make you laugh, cry, gasp or sigh; they can lead you gently along or suddenly push you over a virtual cliff. And, remember they do not call it a lecture *theatre* for nothing. However, if, as a lecturer, you adopt these strategies purely for dramatic effect then they may fall flat. On the other hand, if you choose them carefully and use them only to carry along the narrative of your lecture or to emphasise points and exemplify your arguments, then they can be highly successful. It is often these aspects of a lecture that either label it as a great success or an equally great failure.

EMPATHY

It is always difficult to remember what it was like when you first came to the subject on which you are now lecturing. It is likely to have been years, sometimes decades ago. In order to give your audience the best chance of understanding your lecture, and getting the most from it, you need to be able to put yourself in their place. This may mean trying to understand and share their feelings, and to assume their level of knowledge or ignorance of your subject. This approach will also force you to rethink any assumptions you make.

When the physicist R.V. Jones reflected on his wartime experiences of lecturing RAF personnel he said:

> "Subconsciously I acquired the two secrets of lecturing from which everything else follows: first, to believe that you have something worth telling your audience, and then to imagine yourself as one of that audience. Nearly all the advice that I have seen given to would-be lecturers deals with trimmings without mentioning the fundamentals: but if you get these right, they entail all the rest. You must, for example, talk in terms that appeal to the background experience of your audience. You must be audible at the back of the room, where the details of your lantern slides must be visible and your blackboard writing legible; and you should not distract your audience with antics and fidgeting. You must also

detect by the change in tension when you are in danger of losing its interest. But all these follow from the simple consideration of trying to regard yourself from the point of view of a member of the audience in the back row."

(Jones 1978, quoted in Ramsden 2003)

This 'putting yourself in the back-row' mentality is an essential element of designing and delivering an effective lecture. So many lecturers clearly fail to do this and the consequences are poorly constructed, inappropriately complex or over-simplified, sometimes even patronizing presentations that do not even come close to being useful lectures.

Much of this book has been about attitude. Empathy with your audience is an important aspect of this, and I really cannot emphasise enough that the key to a good lecture is to adopt this habit of thinking about your audience, its attributes, its knowledge and its needs.

WEB RESOURCES

This is a list of websites I have found useful that provide information related to speaking and presenting in its widest sense.

Please remember that websites come and go, reflecting the dynamic nature of the internet. All the sites below were current at the time of writing, but if they have changed their addresses or have disappeared altogether, or worse, have transmuted into sites that carry unsuitable or incorrect content, please do not hold me or the publishers responsible.

www.istockphoto.com

iStockphoto is the internet's original member-generated image and design community. Here you will be able to purchase affordable, royalty-free photographs, vector illustrations, video footage and audio tracks to enhance your presentations.

www.cyborlink.com/

Described as "The Web's leading resource for International Business Etiquette and Manners" this site has a wealth of useful information about most of the countries you are ever likely to visit including sections on cultural dos and don'ts.

www.academic-skills.com

This is a developing site that contains useful information for those wishing to find out more about a range of different academic skills including lecturing, writing, and preparing slides and posters.

www.performanceanxiety.com

This is the website of Janet Esposito who is the author of one of my recommended readings: *In the Spotlight*. On this website you can find out more about her approach to helping people overcome their fear of public speaking.

www.cultivate-int.org/issue3/presentations/

Here you will find some useful tips on slide design and the practical use of PowerPoint.

office.microsoft.com/en-gb/powerpoint/default.aspx

There are of course hundreds of sites that will offer support and advice about the use of Microsoft's PowerPoint software, but this site will lead you to the horse's mouth. Also remember that the online help you can access from within the program itself is often invaluable.

www.toastmasters.org/tips.asp

This site lists 10 quick tips for improving your public speaking and has links to a range of other relevant resources.

www.speaking-tips.com/

This site is authored by an American academic who specialises in speech communication. It contains a wide range of relevant articles that contain a lot of very useful advice. Sections include Ice Breakers, Storytelling, Using Humour, Voice Control, and Giving a Eulogy.

SUGGESTIONS FOR FURTHER READING

Hopefully, after you have read this book, you may be stimulated to read more on the topics discussed here. There are, however, more books written about lecturing, presentation skills, preparing slides and public speaking than it is possible to read in a reasonable lifetime. So where should you begin? Below I have listed some of the many books which you may find interesting. Should you wish to purchase any of these suggested texts you will find them all conveniently listed at the Amazon Bookstores on the following websites **www.allangaw.com** and **www.academic-skills.com**

General Books on Lecturing

Newble D, Cannon R. (2000) A Handbook for Teachers in Universities and Colleges: A Guide to Improving Teaching Methods 4th edition, Routledge, Abingdon.
ISBN-13: 978-0749431815

This is one of the first books I read about lecturing and teaching and remains one of the best. It has been updated and revised several times over the years and it is the one book

I always recommend to new university lecturers, no matter what their discipline.

Issever C and Peach K. (2010) Presenting Science: A Practical Guide to Giving a Good Talk. OUP, Oxford. ISBN-13: 978-0199549092

This is very much aimed at lectures and other forms of presentation in the sciences and in particular physics, where all the examples in the book come from. It has some very useful sections on structuring a scientific presentation with emphasis on presenting mathematical concepts and notation.

Heller R. (2002) High Impact Speeches: How to Create and Deliver Words That Move Minds. Prentice Hall, London. ISBN-13: 978-0273662020

Although not written specifically for those giving lectures there is a wealth of useful information here that anyone having to deliver any form of speech – from a political rally, to an award acceptance, to the PTA, to the keynote address of the International Society of Psychiatrists – would do well to heed. The book is primarily about words – indeed there are no pictures at all – and the use of those words, to argue, convince, sway, and move an audience. There is a very useful section giving real examples of high impact speeches and an analysis of why they work.

Egan M. (1997) Would You Really Rather Die Than Give a Talk? Amacom, New York. ISBN-13: 978-0814479414

This is a book about preparing and giving a business presentation written in the form of a cartoon strip. There is a lot of useful information and helpful tips embedded in this rather unorthodox format and as Oscar Wilde said: "For those who like that sort of thing, it's the sort of thing that they like."

Bachmann N. (2009) Speaking Volumes: Transform Your Business Through Effective Communication. Word4Word, Evesham.
ISBN-13: 978-1906316235

A tiny pocket book of only around 50 small pages which still manages to contain a lot of good, simple advice and some inspiring quotes.

Dealing with Nerves and Fear

Esposito J. (2008) In the Spotlight: Overcome Your Fear of Public Speaking and Performing. Capstone, Chichester.
ISBN-13: 978-1906465117

This book is about stage fright and how to overcome it. Strategies to reduce fear and build confidence are set out, but these take time and effort and therefore commitment from the user. No magic solutions are offered because there aren't any, just solid practical advice. If you have a particularly disabling form of stage fright – remember we are all nervous when we speak – then this book might help.

Antony MM. (2004) 10 Simple Solutions to Shyness. How to Overcome Shyness, Social Anxiety and Fear of Public Speaking. New Harbinger Publications, Oakland.
ISBN-13: 978-1572243484

This is a concise self-help book written by a psychologist with a special interest in treating those with social anxiety. The book is full of useful advice and, as the title suggests, presents ten "simple solutions". (Number nine is entitled: "Learn to make presentations with confidence".) It has a series of practical exercises which, as the author points out, need to be completed thoroughly if you hope to benefit from the approach outlined in the book.

Visual Aids

Duarte N. (2008) slide:ology: The Art and Science of Creating Great Presentations. O'Reilly Media, Inc, Sebastopol.
ISBN-13: 978-0596522346

Nancy Duarte, the author of this book, runs the company that created the presentation for Al Gore's film *An Inconvenient Truth*, proving that you can win not only an Oscar, but also a Nobel Peace Prize, with a great slide show. Her book, therefore, needs little more recommendation, but you will find that it is packed with great ideas and sound advice about slide design and is written on the premise that you should "never deliver a presentation you wouldn't want to sit through."

Reynolds G. (2008) Presentation Zen: Simple Ideas on Presentation Design and Delivery. New Riders, Berkeley.
ISBN-13: 978-0321525659

This book is a simply beautiful object and is full of new (at least new to me) ways of designing slides for more effective presentations. The emphasis is on business presentation, but most of what is included could be easily adapted for other settings. Hundreds of examples are shown in full colour, and even the foreword is presented as a PowerPoint slide show.

Educational Theory

Ramsden P. (2003) Learning to Teach in Higher Education. 2nd edition, RoutledgeFalmer, London.
ISBN-13: 978-0415303453

This is a comprehensive approach to University teaching and has as its basic tenet that "to become a good teacher, first you must understand your students' experience of learning."

While the book covers much more than lecturing it is a valuable source of a great deal of the educational theory that underpins how we teach. Ramsden, however, presents this theory in a thoroughly practical context and I believe that is what makes this book worth reading.

Bligh D. (1998) What's the Use of Lectures? 5th edition, Intellect Books, Bristol.
ISBN-13: 978-1871516791

This book is regarded by many as a classic and is certainly a thoroughly referenced piece of scholarship. It is also readable and full of very practical advice, but its primary use I believe is as an excellent exposition of much of the educational theory that forms the foundation for what we do in lectures.

Cowan J. (2006) On Becoming an Innovative University Teacher. Reflection in Action. 2nd edition, Open University Press, Maidenhead.
ISBN-13: 978-0335219926

Written by an educationalist with an engineering background this book is accessible and easy to read, but is full of detailed educational theory particularly as it relates to effective reflective learning. There is little specifically about lecturing – indeed *lectures* appears once in a 14 page index – but there is much of general interest for those who wish to be better teachers.

Meyers C and Jones TB. (1993) Promoting Active Learning. Strategies for the College Classroom. Jossey-Bass Publishers, San Francisco.
ISBN-13: 978-1555425241

Written by two American humanities professors, this book is about placing the student front and centre in your teaching and promoting active learning rather than passive absorption of information. The authors note in their preface that the book contains no "diatribe against lecturing". Indeed they state that they value lecturing highly, but feel that students also need active learning opportunities.

Body Language

Pease A and Pease B. (2005) The Definitive Book of Body Language: How to Read Others' Attitudes by Their Gestures. Orion, London.
ISBN-13: 978-0752858784

This is a very readable and entertaining account of this topic. As with all books on body language there are sections on courtship and sexual attraction. You probably want to avoid those, especially if you are a University lecturer as there are usually institutional policies in place about that kind of stuff when it comes to your students. However, there are also invaluable sections on the basics as well as interesting sections on cultural differences. Allan Pease, one of the authors, is also a very good lecturer and presenter if you ever get the opportunity to hear him.

Multicultural Etiquette

Morrison T and Conway WA. (2006) Kiss, Bow or Shake Hands: The Bestselling Guide to Doing Business in More Than 60 Countries. 2nd edition, Adams Media Corporation, Avon.
ISBN-13: 978-1593373689

For many this American book is the bible of multicultural manners and will be very useful if you are travelling to any of the 62 countries it covers. It also contains a lot of useful background geographical and geopolitical data for each area.

Axtell RE. (1993) Do's and Taboos around the World. 3rd edition, John Wiley & Sons, New York.
ISBN-13: 978-0471595281

This is another American book, but much shorter although inevitably less comprehensive, than Morrison and Conway. Here the topic is very much presented in an entertaining and humorous way with lots of fascinating stories.

Facilitation

Chambers R. (2002) Participatory Workshops: A Sourcebook of 21 Sets of Ideas and Activities. Earthscan Ltd, London.
ISBN-13: 978-1853838637

This is a sourcebook for presenters and facilitators. Many of the approaches are not immediately applicable to the conventional lecture setting, but if you are facilitating workshops or training sessions you will find a lot of useful suggestions here, including "21 Tips on How to Avoid Lecturing."

Sims NH. (2006) How to Run a Great Workshop: The Complete Guide to Designing and Running Brilliant Workshops and Meetings. Pearson Education Ltd, Harlow.
ISBN-13: 978-0273707875

This book is described as a "quick fix solution to running successful group sessions" and is presented in a very accessible format. It provides many good suggestions for facilitators, especially if they are new to this task.

INDEX